Norma Brophy was born on the back of a horse-drawn wagon in 1936. She spent her youth travelling Australia with her hard-working showmen family, learning carpentry, signwriting, costume design and spruiking, with a short foray as a stunt motorbike rider. Later, with her husband Mick and five children, Norma worked all aspects of show business and circus including as a spruiker, snake handler, 'psychic medium' and circus owner. Norma hung up her ringmaster's hat after managing her children's world-record-breaking acrobatic act, The Flying Angels. Today Norma's paintings of show history on tent canvas are considered valuable records of Australian history, www.carnivalart.com.au. She lives in Brisbane.

Wendy Stuart is a freelance editor and wordsmith based in Queensland. She enjoyed working collaboratively with 'Aunty' Norma over several years in developing *Don't Call Us Carnies*. Since founding Wendy & Words in 2010, Wendy has edited over sixty non-fiction books. She is a Professional Member of the Institute of Professional Editors.

NORMA BROPHY *WITH* WENDY STUART

Published by Affirm Press in 2022
28 Thistlethwaite Street, South Melbourne
Boonwurrung Country, VIC 3205
affirmpress.com.au
10 9 8 7 6 5 4 3 2 1

A catalogue record for this book is available from the National Library of Australia

Title: Don't Call Us Carnies / Norma Brophy with Wendy Stuart, authors.
ISBN: 9781922626851 (paperback)

Cover design by Josh Durham/Design by Committee
Typeset in Minion Pro by J&M Typesetting
Proudly printed in Australia by Griffin Press

In loving memory of my husband Alfred (Mick) Roy Brophy

and dedicated to my people – the show people.

A Word from the Author

I am one of the last of the older show people. My family's involvement in the business goes back many generations. Since the 1850s, we showfolk have travelled the length and breadth of this massive country, bringing wonders and delights that many Australians had never before seen or dreamed of. I am so proud to have been a part of such a marvellous industry.

We are often called 'carnies'. The term originates from the 1920s, when American carnivals were infiltrated by sleight-of-hand con artists. These shysters became known as 'carnies'. But please, don't call us that. We're 'showies' – showmen – and damn proud of it!

I was born a showie. Everyone outside our community was a 'local'. I still see myself as a showie, even though I am settled down in retirement. It was only in these later years that I came to realise that my 'local' friends were fascinated by my life. At first, I couldn't understand why. But as my friends pointed out, many people dream of joining a circus or a show.

As a child, I never thought my life was unusual. But it was. On show days, we ran wild. All the rides and sideshows were free for us. If we show kids were mates with the canteen kids, we also had all the fairy floss, toffee apples and Dagwood dogs we could eat. As we got older, it was normal for us to work on show days. That way, our parents knew exactly where we were. I never questioned it.

As a showie, I have taken on many roles: stunt motorbike rider, truck driver, snake handler, spruiker, fortune teller and nightclub owner. My children have followed in my footsteps as successful show entrepreneurs and world-record-breaking entertainers.

In retirement, I became an artist, painting scenes from the lives of the travelling outdoor entertainers. I was filled with pride when the National Library of Australia invited me to have my website featuring all my present and future paintings preserved in their Pandora Archive. They told me my work needed to be preserved as a treasured piece of Australian history. This prompted me to finally put pen to paper to tell this story.

In researching this book, I have explored many all-but-forgotten moments in our show business history. Some of what I have recorded is family lore, handed down across generations, often around the campfire and over a cup of billy tea.

But this isn't just the story of my own show lineage. It is a tribute to the colourful lives of the many travelling show people and circus and rodeo folk who have contributed so much to our beautiful country as they travelled long and often difficult roads to bring entertainment to the outback.

Through this book you will see where this crazy life can lead us – and believe me, there have been some insane twists and turns in mine. It's no surprise that the theme of my life has been 'The show must go on.'

Would you have enjoyed my life, or would you have just stuck to yours? Read on and decide for yourself.

Contents

Prologue

1951 – Maryborough, Queensland

The 'boys' were all in a pub near the showgrounds one evening when the door was flung wide open. A hulking man from Sharman's Boxing Troupe staggered in, fists clenched, eyeballing the crowd.

'I'll fight any man in the f---in' bar!' he shouted. He'd been on a drinking binge and was in a foul mood, ready to take on the world.

Amid the shouting and laughter, a showman by the name of Mick Brophy stepped forward to accept the challenge.

Word travelled fast round our camp. Some kids came running, yelling about a showie who was crazy enough to take on one of Sharman's biggest boxers.

I was only fourteen years old at the time, but I remember what happened next as clear as a bell. It was the first time I set eyes on my future husband.

A crowd had gathered on a grassy patch near the public bar. With anticipation running high, everyone was having a grouse time. The big, drunk boxer was Ronnie, one of the lead fighters from

Jimmy Sharman's Boxing Tent. He stood over 6 feet tall and seemed just as wide. Mick was just on six feet, but nowhere near as heavy as his opponent.

There was a lot of horsing around in the lead-up, with the men stripping off to the waist. Mick was laughing, dancing around and punching at shadows. Both contenders were being kept well primed with alcoholic beverages.

The show people jammed in close, shouting encouragement. The hulking Ronnie was frothing at the mouth as Mick danced around him, throwing pretend punches and teasing the big fellow almost beyond endurance. Then, with no warning, Ronnie lunged at Mick with a punch that connected. Mick reeled and righted himself. It was on. Amid the screams and yells, the raging Goliath had drawn first blood.

The two men went round for round, trading punches. The stench of sweat was almost overpowering, intermingled with grunts and the thud of knuckles slamming into bare flesh. The screams and yells of the crowd only added to the furore. Neither man would give in. What had started as a drunken bare-knuckle game turned into an hour-long fight to the bitter end.

The pair could not be stopped even when their mates tried to pull them apart. They fought on until they were both on their knees, bloodied from head to foot. There were no more rounds, just continuous slugging.

The crowd had fallen silent. These two fighting machines were trading punch for punch. Finally, in a state of collapse, they were separated. It was a fight like no other, and one that nobody present wanted to see again. It was raw and bloody fury, with no rhyme or reason to it.

Watching on in horror, I could never have imagined that I was going to devote my adult life to one of these men – or that that man would first spend four years in a mental hospital.

As for me, rather than joining the circus, I was about to run away from it.

Chapter 1

The Bibby Bros Show Is Born

1900 – Wellington, New Zealand

'Look at 'em go!' shouted sixteen-year-old Bert Bibby. This man who would be my father was still in his teens, whooping it up with his two younger brothers at a buckjumping show. Having soaked up the sights and sounds of the parade, the three brothers – Bert, John and Ted – were sitting on a bench, cheering on the roughriders who clung to bucking horses for a living.

When the call went out for volunteers to try their luck on one of these bucking brumbies, John Bibby's hand shot up. He was soon hanging on for dear life while the audience cheered him on. John was the only rider from the crowd to stay on for more than five seconds. He managed a good minute. He was one hell of a horseman. His brothers were too, having grown up with horses on their father's farm.

After John's heroics, the Bibby boys settled in to watch the rest of the show. Ted was especially interested in the rope spinners, who twirled their ropes into almost impossible loops. He'd been practising back at the family farm and had started plaiting his first whip.

Next up was a sharpshooter, who calmly blasted a stick of chalk from the hand of his lovely lady assistant. This performance caught the eye of Bert, who was a crack of a shot. 'I'm going to try that one!' he declared.

The three youths spent all their free time visiting the buckjumping shows that toured New Zealand in the early 1900s. They longed to become part of this glamorous show life, a world away from the daily grind of farm life.

After their father, John Snr, died and the farm was sold, the three boys became tent hands and general dogsbodies at their beloved buckjumping events. While honing their rodeo, sharpshooting and rope skills, they grew from lanky teenagers into powerful young men. Their dream remained the same: to start their own buckjump show.

Eventually, they managed to scrape together enough gear to establish a small open-air buckjump show, padded out with circus clowns. The Bibby Bros Buckjump Show debuted in the brothers' hometown of Karori, near Wellington, in May 1903. They performed their buckjumping acts to thunderous applause from paying customers, friends and family who filled the high-tiered timber seating boards surrounding the arena. There was no tent – only hessian partitions with canvas tarpaulins stretched overhead.

Though in ill health, Mary Bibby was proud of her enterprising sons. Their show was no doubt a memory she took with her to her grave a few months later. She was buried in the Karori cemetery.

With both parents gone, the brothers battled on against mounting odds, with the worst being the inclement weather and travelling conditions. Moving the circus from town to town called for a mountain of packing on two heavy-duty wagons, a legacy of their family farming days. There was not only the seating framework and tarps but also the fences and crushes for the buckjumpers, along with the saddles and assorted camping equipment. Audiences seemed willing to cram in under tarpaulins even when wet through to their skin, but this couldn't continue, especially in extreme weather conditions.

For three years, the Bibby boys pressed on, performing in all kinds of weather. In their downtime, they began the challenging work of constructing their first proper show tent. Their sisters and other family members all helped, working from their homes to stitch together more than 1000 yards (914 metres) of marine calico, known as sail cloth.

Once all the sections of the canvas covering were complete, they were laced together. This formed the sharply peaked roof of the circus tent, around which the sidewalls were hooked. Once erected, the tent weighed nearly two tonnes, including the two massive timber 'king poles', guy ropes and pegs.

With the tent hoisted, the show hit new heights. Renamed The Bibby Bros Buckjumping and Circus Show, it featured knife-throwing, whip-cracking, sharpshooting, juggling, tumbling and clowns, to the delight of audiences all over New Zealand.

Fuelled by their success, the brothers felt the call to expand even more. New Zealand was too small for their ambitions. They were ready to tackle the vast continent of Australia. Sure, there were a few rivals across the Ditch, like Skuthorpe's Buckjumping Show and Wirth's Circus, but the brothers had already proved they liked a challenge. And besides, they had a few tricks up their sleeves.

Skuthorpe's Leap

Lance Skuthorpe (1870–1958), one of the craziest of daredevil roughriders, decided in 1900 to re-enact a death-defying stunt. Back in 1864, a well-known poet and writer of verse named Adam Lindsay Gordon had performed a near suicidal feat of horsemanship by jumping his horse, Red Lancer, onto a narrow ledge high above Mount Gambier's Blue Lake in South Australia. This event became known as Gordon's Leap, and an obelisk marks the spot where it took place.

Thirty-six years later, Skuthorpe, while on a visit to the gap, took up the challenge to repeat Gordon's Leap. On a borrowed horse, he spurred his steed forward. They jumped high over the old post-and-rail safety fence and down onto the narrow ledge, a few feet below the roadway (and well over 100 feet above the lake). Man and beast then sprang back up onto the roadway, once again clearing the safety fence. This near-impossible feat has never again been attempted.

Sailing for Sydney aboard the steamer *Monawai* in April 1906, Bert, John and Ted hatched a plan for a show that would take Australia by storm.

On arrival, having freighted their tent and best-performing horses along with them, the Bibby boys set about buying the draft horses needed to pull the wagons. They also snapped up several wild, unrideable horses to use as buckjumpers in their show.

After weeks of preparation, the troupe headed west to perform their first Australian show, in Parramatta.

As ringmaster, Bert led a lively parade down Parramatta Road. The roughriders wore their best cowboy gear: chunky boots, leather chaps, fancy vests and not forgetting their high-crowned Stetson hats. They cracked whips and spun ropes in fancy whirls. Onlookers were just as dazzled by the troupe's beautiful girls in their colourful costumes riding palomino ponies, while clowns and tumblers performed 'flip flaps' (somersaults) up and down the roadway. Behind them came the performing horses, decked out in wonderful, feathered headdresses. They tossed their heads and lifted their legs high, marching in time to the band. As the parade wound its way through the town, it was followed by the local children, all hoping to join in the fun.

Under a jam-packed big top, Ringmaster Bert kicked off the milestone Parramatta show with his knife-throwing act. He was a brilliant marksman and could handle any type of weapon. After setting his assistant Lucy against the target board, he demonstrated the sharpness of his twelve-inch, razor-sharp hunting knives by slicing clean through several sweet melons in one sweep. Whoosh! Much to their delight, the kids in the audience were treated to the freshly sliced melons. Then, when Lucy called 'Ready!', the crowd held its collective breath as Bert hurled a hunting knife her way. Bang! It pierced the board with deadly accuracy, barely missing his lovely assistant. Amid screams and oohs and aahs from the mesmerised crowd, Bert swiftly threw the rest of the knives, outlining Lucy's body. The audience roared with approval, though the act wasn't quite over.

For his finale, Bert was blindfolded. Lucy now turned side-on, with a balloon between her teeth. She didn't even flinch as a knife burst the balloon and plunged deep into the target board behind her – barely a whisker from Lucy's ruby red lips. Amid wild applause, Bert and Lucy took their bows.

Next up was Ted, the expert whip cracker, calling for a volunteer from the audience. A young fellow bravely stepped up and was given a farthing coin (quarter of a penny) to hold in the air. Ted then, with great aplomb, unfurled his long whip and flicked the coin from the lad's hand. The deserving young fellow got to keep the farthing. Next, using a whip in each hand, Ted cut strips of paper that were held aloft by wide-eyed young audience members.

Ted finished with a rope-spinning act in which he twirled a 100-foot (33-metre) rope around his body while standing on his horse's saddle. The crowds loved it.

Then came John. Though a born troublemaker, often getting into bar-room fights and being arrested for affray, he was a saint on horseback. He entered the arena riding bareback on Black Bob – a glistening, jet black three-year-old stallion trained by John. After circling wide and high-stepping beautifully, Black Bob exploded into action, bucking and stampeding while John stuck like glue to his back. The stunned onlookers almost fell from their seats at this unexpected display.

Dismounting mid-flight, John settled the seemingly wild horse. With a wave of John's hand, Black Bob bent on one knee and bowed to the appreciative crowd.

Local wannabe cowboys were then called upon to have a go at riding one of the Bibbys' buckjumping horses. Few stayed on long. This was followed by crazy circus clowns, balancing artists, jugglers and trick ponies that amazed the audience with their almost human antics, all rounded off with a three-piece band of accordion, guitar and mouth organ.

Ringmaster Bert announced the next act by calling for another youngster from the audience – this time to ride the buckjumping donkey. Try as they might, dozens of horrified parents couldn't stop their kids from waving, yelling and pleading, 'Pick me! Pick me!'

With one brave boy chosen, the donkey was led into the arena. A leather safety belt was strapped around the lad's waist, with a connecting rope threaded through a pulley at the top of the king pole. The young 'bronc buster' was lifted astride his steed, then, with a slap on the rump, the donkey came alive, bolting and jolting as his young rider clung on for dear life. Just as the daring young cowboy looked done for, he found himself lifted high above the arena, virtually swimming in mid-air, arms and legs flailing in all directions. Meanwhile, far below, a now placid donkey was calmly munching on a handful of straw.

Amid the cheers and laughter, the young rider was brought back to earth and rewarded with a toffee apple.

The show was a resounding success. The Bibby brothers had made their mark in Australia, but it was only the first step on a wild, and ultimately heartbreaking, journey.

Chapter 2

The Show on the Road

Circa 1908

The next stop for the Bibby brothers was Victoria. With gold still being mined around places like Bendigo and Ballarat, there was money to be earned throughout this region. Having kept their show relatively compact, the troupe was well drilled and could travel fast, visiting smaller towns that were overlooked by the larger circus shows. For the next few years, they travelled all around the state, stopping for a few days in each town.

With the hitching up of the horses a big part of each moving day, things didn't always go to plan. One time, with the wagons all packed and ready to go, Bert tried to move the first set of horses into the traces, but the beasts wouldn't budge. He gave each one a good slap on the rump. That'll fix 'em. But they still wouldn't move. Bert's only option was to take the stubborn blighters for a walk, holding firmly to the halters. Finally, he had them ambling along quietly. But as soon as he headed them back to the wagon, all hell broke loose. The mongrels bolted, and Bert landed on his bum. Oh, well. Just another day in the life of a circus man.

On a good moving day, the horses averaged 7 miles (11 kilometres) an hour. At that pace, it could take almost a fortnight to get from town to town.

Even packed away, the show was quite a sight. Three wagons, pulled by six horses each, were required for the big-top tent alone. Several more wagons were needed for the arena fences, crushes (chutes for holding and releasing bucking horses into the arena), tiered timber bench seating, saddles and sundry equipment. Another wagon carried feed for the working horses on long hauls when roadside grass was sparse.

The next wagon was the cookhouse, possibly the most important wagon of the lot, which carried two huge water barrels. The living wagons added up to at least another five, with a small two-horse wagon for the advance man to travel ahead of the show to organise sites and put up posters advertising the Bibby Bros' forthcoming show. All in all, fourteen wagons with a minimum of sixty horses were needed.

Being herded along after the wagons were the buckjumpers and trick ponies, along with at least fifty spare relief horses – a total of 130 head. To keep all of this on the move there were the workmen, roughriders (cowboys) and clowns, jugglers and performing dogs.

Drinking water could be hard to come by on the road. Unless you managed to get some tank water from a friendly local, it was creeks and rivers. By adding a spoonful of Epsom salts to a bucket of river water, the mud would settle overnight, leaving crystal clear water. As these salts could have a laxative effect, it was important not to use too much. Toilets were few and far between out in the back country!

Needless to say, proper bathing facilities were non-existent. A bird bath was sometimes the best that could be had, better known as a 'lick and a promise'. Using a dish of water, you started at the top and worked your way to the bottom. Your feet were always last, oh, and you didn't forget the middle part!

Bert made sure the cook had a Coolgardie safe. This was a small box-type cupboard made of wire mesh, covered with a wet hessian bag. Fitted with a hook on the top, it could be hung from a tree branch, away from ants and the blowies. When a breeze came, it would pass through the hessian and cool the food inside. The Coolgardie was especially good for storing the sheep meat that the travelling show folk 'found' along the way. Thank goodness there was plenty of 'wild' sheep around. For more legitimate tucker, they turned to the rivers and creeks, where the fishing was often good, along with the duck hunting.

A simple method was used to catch ducks: a fishing line or length of string was threaded through a hole in a big rat trap. The trap was then baited with some fat off a piece of meat and set to float in the water. A half dozen traps could be set this way and, by morning, there would be the makings of a feast fit for a king. If the troupe was lucky enough to be near a town with a railway line, they could also have vegies and fruit to go with their mains. Once a fortnight or so, the train came through with fresh – well, sometimes not so fresh – produce. Either way, a stock-up of supplies was made. Then the cook would go to work.

A favourite camp-oven meal was leg of 'wild' sheep, with roast potatoes, pumpkin, cabbage and gravy. There could be an apple pie or baked damper hot from the fire's coals, with plenty of butter made from the cream skimmed off the rich milk that the 'wild' cow gave you yesterday.

No matter what was on the menu, the cookhouse campfire drew a crowd. At the end of a long day of travel, the show families would unpack and wander over with their kids, carrying stools or boxes to sit on. Inevitably, someone would start yarning over dinner about the day's trek and the troubles on the road. This would lead into an endless supply of tall stories, sometimes about a 'monster fish' that got away or a good-looking girl who did the same. With billy tea and conversation flowing, the hot coals could be used to roast spuds, which were smothered in homemade butter and sprinkled with salt and pepper.

The circus women were brilliant cooks. But keeping everyone fed was only part of the never-ending job. They made and maintained all the beautiful costumes needed to add glamour to the show. As well as handling and grooming the trick horses, they worked in the arena as assistants to the sharpshooters, or even as lady roughriders. They also bore the children who were the up-and-coming performers. Oh, and added to all that, they were the ticket sellers. These were tough women with hearts of gold, who worked as hard as any man. The strange thing about all this was that everyone retained their sense of humour, with a ready smile for all. And then, when show night arrived, it was almost with a sense of relief. 'Whew, now we can relax.'

Over the next few years, the Bibby Bros occasionally operated a sideshow at the smaller one-day agricultural shows, offering shortened half-hour versions of their buckjumping routines. As there was no electricity, these shows were held during daylight hours only.

Bert and his brothers had quickly worked out that these agricultural shows had readymade audiences. The farming community would come to town for the day, then stay the night to see the Bibby Bros' full two-hour buckjump show, where the tent and show arena were lit up by carbide lamps. These huge lamps were used by train engines to light up the tracks at night. The lamps had an adjustable upper and lower chamber, allowing water droplets from the upper chamber to mix with the calcium carbide in the lower chamber. This formed a highly ignitable gas called acetylene that gave out a brilliant light. The downside was the smell; rotting fish could not be more pungent. (It would not be until 1912 that a new light would become available, called the 'glory light'. This was a tank filled with petrol into which air was pumped until it reached around 40 pounds (18 kilograms) of pressure. This then formed a gas that was channelled to lamps placed around the arena. They were a good light, and much safer than the highly ignitable carbide lamps.)

When the night-time show was finished and the show folk

were winding down, they'd settle around the campfire together. On nights such as these, with everyone pleasantly weary, one of the old roustabouts would step up to tell stories. Charlie, a great orator, loved to thrill – or terrify – the children with his tales of ghosts and ghouls. Kids with full bellies snuggled up in their mother's arms, eyes popping, as Charlie weaved a yarn. Like this one:

The Tale of the Man Who Lost his Head

There once was a lonely man who lived in a little house out the back of Bourke. His only mate was a pet kangaroo. One night, a bad storm started. The wind howled and there was thunder, lightning and rain. Very frightened, the man curled up tight in his bed. When he woke the next morning, his pet roo asked him, 'What did you do with your head?' Puzzled, the man felt all around and found his head right down at the bottom of the bed, under the blankets. Snatching it up, the man stumbled out of the house, with the roo close behind. 'I have to find a doctor!' the head yelled.

But there was no doctor to be found in Bourke. The man knew he had to move on to a larger town for help. With his head tucked firmly under his arm and his pet roo hopping along beside him to show the way, the man continued his long and dreadfully lonely journey south, through the dry and dusty wind-torn plains of outback New South Wales. Wherever he went, people ran from him in terror at the sight of a headless man and his kangaroo.

The strange pair blundered on for hundreds of miles, eventually arriving at Broken Hill. Here, the people chased the headless man out of town, shouting, 'You're a freak! You're a freak! Go away!'

The headless man and his pet kangaroo had no choice but to keep going. They followed the endless roads alone and weary, forever looking for help that would never come. They say they're out there still.

Stories like this would leave the kids gaping. They would be staring out into the darkness, expecting the headless man and his roo to appear at any moment. With his audience captivated, the storyteller might follow up with the tale of the ghost that floated through the bush surrounding the circus camps. He'd point to the shrubbery, waving his arms and working up all kinds of frightening moans and groans. By this point, the youngsters would be goggle-eyed, convinced a ghost was about to float their way from the shadowy shrubbery. 'Wooooooo!'

These stories inevitably ended with gentle laughter as the parents bundled their jittery kids off to bed, and the guitarist softly strummed a lullaby. The adults would then chuck ideas around the fire as to how to improve the show.

Unlike the bigger, more established outfits, the Bibby Bros Buckjump & Circus Show of 1908 was not a traditional circus with trapeze artists, contortionists, acrobats and high-rope walkers. With their tent already rotting away from mildew, and no money to fix it, they were in dire need of more drawcards. But what act would really stand out? Bert, his brothers and fellow performers were at a loss to come up with one. It was almost as if they were waiting for something to fly out of the sky. As luck would have it, that's pretty much what happened.

Just as the Bibby brothers were losing hope of finding an act that would set their fledgling show apart, a new act found them. Out of the blue, two young American performers wandered into camp. They were brothers Robert and John Smithson. They had a cannon act, which had been left behind when the stunt show they worked for headed back to the United States without them. Now, they were desperate for work.

As luck would have it, the Bibbys' weather-beaten big top tent had rotted away so badly that the arena was now an open-air arrangement – making it a suitable launching pad for a human cannonball.

The first time the brothers demonstrated their act in the arena, the tension among the circus people was magnetic. With Robert loaded into the cylinder, John pretended to light a fuse with a flaming torch. (It was in fact just a fuse with no explosive properties.) Then, with a loud blast (some good sound effects!), the cannon erupted to the horrified screams of seasoned show folk. Out flew Robert with immense force, propelled by compressed air. He somersaulted through the air at great speed, up and up, through the opening in the tent roof, and out of sight. The onlookers gasped. How could he possibly have survived that? A moment later, Robert strolled through the front door and took a bow. Having landed squarely in a specially constructed net outside the big top, this amazing flyer was none the worse for the mind-shattering experience. With that, Bibby Bros had one of the first human cannonball acts to travel the east coast of Australia.

This high-flying act was such a ticket-boosting crowd pleaser that the Bibby big top soon became known as the Cannon Top Tent. The Bibbys were on a winner. For several years, the cannon act went off without a hitch. Until one night, when Robert somersaulted into the sky and out of sight, without returning. After an agonising wait, someone raced outside to check the safety net; there was no sign of the young man. The entire audience was assembled to look for the missing flyer. Fire torches were provided, and the search began. Any last hope of finding Robert alive was all but gone when a faint voice was heard in the distant darkness. 'Help me …' It was Robert! He had overshot the safety net and landed high in a gum tree! He was tangled up and semi-conscious. Quite seriously hurt. But he would live to tell the tale.

That was the last straw for the Smithson brothers. There had been a few close calls in the past, but the gum tree landing was by far the worst. On Robert's recovery, the pair gave away show business. They sold their cannon to Wirth's Circus and returned home to America, seen off with a big farewell party by the Bibby Bros.

Chapter 3

Bert and Florence

1909–1912

On a triumphant return to New Zealand in 1909, the Bibby brothers unveiled a new hair-raising act, billed as 'The Great Globe of Death'. Inside a gigantic sphere of steel mesh, a man and a woman rode pushbikes in hurtling loops. The lady rider then swapped her bike for a miniature car, while the man switched to a motorbike. With motors revving, the car and the motorcycle looped the loop, racing, riding, dipping and diving – missing each other by bare inches. Audiences loved it!

In the weeks before Christmas, while setting up for a new show in Auckland, Bert spied an enchanting sixteen-year-old local named Florence. He was soon enamoured with her. Florence's hotel publican father, Joseph Burke, didn't approve of this circus man who was ten years older than his precious daughter. But he was fighting a losing battle. Florence was besotted with Bert, and the idea of being a circus woman. She jumped at the chance to wear pretty costumes as an assistant in front of cheering audiences. What a magic life, cooking on an open fire and living in a wagon pulled by two huge horses as they travelled from town to town.

The happy couple were married in January 1910. In September of that year, to Bert's great delight, Florence gave birth to a daughter, Edna Mariana Bibby. But Florence was learning very quickly that the life of a circus woman in the back of a wagon was not the bed of roses she had envisioned. The magic was wearing off, fast, especially after this next incident.

One day, at the beginning of winter 1912, the Bibby Bros were heading to their winter quarters to wait out the coldest months of the year. Florence was due to have a second baby within weeks and had her hands full with Edna. The almost-two-year-old was climbing all around as Florence struggled to keep the wagon horses moving on the slippery, muddy track. Bert was off on his horse leading the procession.

Finally, Florence had had enough and with a swift slap to Edna's bottom, the naughty girl was sent to bed in the back of the wagon. It was a dreary day of cold, intermittent rain and Edna drifted off, rocked to sleep by the movement of the wagon on the rough road. Florence could at last drive the wagon in peace and safety.

When the show wagons reached their campsite, Florence went to check on Edna. She was gone! Florence shrieked and called out to Bert. The wagon was searched thoroughly but there was no sign of the little girl. Florence sobbed uncontrollably and started blaming herself.

Bert quickly got a search party together. With darkness falling, there was no time to contemplate the unthinkable. With lanterns lit, the horsemen started searching the road and shrubbery back along the way they had come. The men grew hoarse from calling out – Bert the loudest. Still there was no sign of the tiny girl. Eventually Bert called them all to a halt. He said they needed to head back and search the roadside more thoroughly. Suddenly, one of the men thought he heard a faint sound ahead of them. 'Quiet! I can hear something.'

They all kept their horses still and strained their ears. From the distance came a faint, 'Dadda, Dadda!'

'There she is!' They had found little Edna, her little white dress covered in sticky black mud, crawling along in the furrow made by the wagon wheels.

Edna was too young to explain what had happened to her. But her parents later surmised that, on waking, she must have struggled down to the foot of the bed to see what was outside and been flipped off the wagon, perhaps by a sudden jerk on the rough road.

After this awful scare, Florence was all the more disillusioned with life on the road, which was made no easier with the arrival of Edna's little brother, Francis (Frank) Albert Bibby.

By the end of 1912, the Bibby circus extravaganza had covered both the north and south islands of New Zealand. Once again, Australia beckoned. The show and its entourage sailed directly to Tasmania, opening in Hobart for a four-week season in the new year. From there, they made a country run of the smaller towns.

As winter made the Tasmanian roads impassable, talk turned to touring the mainland.

But when Florence got wind of these plans, she put her foot down.

'I am not going to live any longer in a wagon, Bert!' she shouted. She was nineteen years old, with two young children in tow, and she wanted a house she could call her own. 'I want a home without wheels that my children can't fall out of! I want my child to grow up in a civilised community!'

After many tears, Florence told Bert he could continue to travel with the circus, under certain conditions. She had it all worked out. He was to buy a house for her in Launceston. And he was to send a monthly sum of money from the circus for her and the children to live on.

The Bibby brothers were relatively well off. As Bert saw it, buying a house would be a good investment, personally and professionally. After a brief search, Florence fell in love with a house in James Street, Launceston. This was the home she wanted to raise her kids in.

With Bert's young family settled into their new place, the Bibby brothers set sail for Melbourne in September 1913. After showing at various towns, Bert ducked back across Bass Strait for a Christmas break with his wife and kids before continuing the tour into New South Wales.

Bert missed his little family but was happy to be back on the road. Reaching Goondiwindi, on the Queensland border, he got a letter from Florence with some big news. She was once again pregnant. The baby was due in September, 1914. There was no way he could be back in Tasmania for the birth as the circus would be well into Queensland by then. Florence would have to handle this herself. *It's her bloody fault*, thought Bert. *She wanted to live in a house!*

By August, with the show in Rockhampton, word was spreading that Australia was getting tangled up in a war on the other side of the world. From Bert's point of view, it was someone else's battle, but Ted and John were excited about it. They said they were tired of the circus life and wanted to call it quits. They wanted to join the army and see the world.

'Bloody idiots!' fumed Bert. 'You'll all get your blinking heads blown off!'

With talk of war putting everyone on edge, Bert decided they would head south to Brisbane for some time off. Having heard no further news from Florence, he was also starting to worry about how she was going. When he finally got to see his young wife, it was with a heavy heart. Florence had suffered a great deal of stress while carrying their third child, and the poor bub had been stillborn several weeks earlier. Florence was depressed and refusing to leave the house. She didn't want to see her neighbours or even the midwife. She told Bert she wanted to leave Tasmania as it held too many unhappy memories.

The circus was still resting up in Brisbane, so Bert felt the best idea would be to move his family up there, pointing out to Florence that it would be a great place for the kids. Plus, he would be able to come home more often as he could work the circus mostly around Brisbane.

Over the following months, Bert shifted his family into a lovely house in Annerley, in suburban Brisbane. And Florence? She seemed happier to Bert. What he didn't know was that his wife was holding a secret that wouldn't be revealed for another seventy years.

Chapter 4

End of an Era

1915

By 1915, World War I was raging in Europe. Across the globe, lives and livelihoods were in turmoil. A vast number of young Australians were rushing to join up; there was even talk of conscription. Among the recruits were Ted and John Bibby. What was older brother Bert to do? The Bibby brothers' circus had run for twelve years, but now it was doomed. He couldn't run the whole operation on his own; he had to sell. He felt gutted but had no other option.

Bert reluctantly struck a deal with giant rival Wirth's Circus, who were keen to snap up the Bibbys' Great Globe of Death act. The daredevils would fit nicely in Wirth's enormous 2000-seat marquee. The big-name circus also bought the Bibbys' open-top tent to use as an animal menagerie to exhibit their performing animals. The biggest benefit would be that all the Bibby Bros performing horses would be well cared for.

The Bibbys' buckjumping horses and load-carrying wagons were sold off to Skuthorpe's Royal Buckjump Show (later Skuthorpe's Wild Australia). Famed roughrider Lance Skuthorpe and his family were long-time competitors to Bibby Bros, and they were naturally interested in adding the prized Bibby Bros horses to their show. With a fair price agreed on, Skuthorpe's added some beaut beasts and wagons to their show. The rest of the wagons and equipment would be sold off over the coming years. For Bert and his brothers, the dream was over. Bibby Bros Buckjump & Circus show was no more.

Taking up a factory job, Bert tried to settle into life in Brisbane as a regular family man. But after a few months, he began to feel stifled. He did not take kindly to punching a time clock, or being ordered around by the factory boss. He missed his horses and the company of men of his own creed. His marriage was suffering; something had to give.

Salvation arrived in the form of an army advertisement. As part of the war effort, thousands of horses were needed by the ANZAC Mounted Division in Egypt. Many had already been commandeered and shipped overseas by the army, irrespective of whether they were used to pulling wagons or performing for adoring crowds. This had brought several circuses, buckjump shows and carnivals to a halt, with no hope of compensation from the government. Some of these companies would never open again.

With the army offering good prices for horses in a rideable condition, Bert saw a golden opportunity to flee his factory job, and make a 'wad of money' for his family. He soon won himself a contract to find and deliver a thousand brumbies, broken to saddle. He was to round them up in outback South Australia and muster them to the coast, for shipping out from Port Augusta. High-spirited ferals that run wild in the back blocks of Australia, brumbies are descendants of escaped or lost horses. Bert was confident that when broke to saddle, these creatures would quickly become valuable assets.

Bert tracked down five of his toughest old-time roughriders. With a string of good riding horses, they loaded as much food and equipment as they could onto pack horses. It was not a good time to go bush – summer was on the way and temperatures were already creeping up – but for Bert and his men there was no choice in the matter. The Australian Army was counting on them – and they were going to earn a good few quid in lean times.

For this story, dear reader, I ask you to jump in the saddle and ride along with me. This is a tale best told in my father's own words, just the way he used to tell it to us around the campfire over the years.

The Brumby War Horses

My mates and me left Brisbane just as day was breaking, late in August 1915. We headed west to Toowoomba. From there, we followed a bush track to Cecil Plains homestead and then on to Moonie, a bit of a dump but a good stop-over to rest. From there it was a fair trek to St George.

This was the land of wide-open spaces, teeming with emus, roos, dingos and cattle, all roaming free. We weren't pushing it as it was bloody hot, and everyone we met wanted to know all the war news. It was a long haul to Cunnamulla, on the way to nowhere. After many weeks on the track, it was time for a break. We stopped at a homestead to rest our horses, and our bloody sore bums. While there, we handed round a bundle of newspapers that we had brought with us to let the homesteaders look through.

Cunnamulla is in the middle of the huge dry plains country of outback Queensland – dry as a dog's bone. The town sits on a crossroads: south to Bourke, north to Charleville, east to where we came from and west to not much at all – which is where we were heading.

As luck had it, there was a picture-show man in town when we arrived. We decided we'd stay for the week. The boys weren't going to miss the movies, and the chance of seeing grouse-looking sheilas, before tackling some of the worst bastards of so-called roads ever made in Australia. These tracks were built only for horses and wagons and sometimes not even for them. We were carrying all our water in canvas water bags as creeks were few and far between in this arid country.

In the early part of our ride, we had been well fed at the homesteads where we had stopped. 'Bog in, boys,' they'd say. But from Cunnamulla on, we'd have to live off the land, eating roos, rabbits and anything else that flew, jumped and slithered.

From Cunnamulla we continued west to Thargomindah, the end of the road. It only had a shed for an outpost. Then, on a hardly used track, we went on to Cameron Corner, which had no town at all and only a surveyor's wooden post to show us where we were. This is the point where Queensland, New South Wales and South Australia meet.

Reaching Callabonna Creek over the border in South Australia, we got to work setting up a permanent camp. From this spot, we could drive our herds of brumbies south, following the creeks and rivers all the way to Port Augusta. The army would then take them off our hands and ship them to Egypt, after paying us a bucket-load of cash on the barrel head.

The Indigenous people in the area were very friendly. Some had worked on nearby stations and were pretty fair horsemen. In fact, we couldn't have done the job without them.

They had a camp of women and kids away back along the creek. The women often brought us bush tucker. For the first time, we tasted yams, which looked a bit like rough-skinned sweet potatoes and tasted pepperish when roasted in the coals. For greens, we were treated to the leaves of a type of thistle that tasted like spinach. With lots of berries, wombats and goannas, the men and I were well fed.

Sitting around the fire at night, on the banks of the Callabonna, we could hear sounds that you only hear in the bush. The quiet gurgle of fish that occasionally flopped about in the water, the muted call of birds heading home and the smell of damper cooking on the coals. Yes, this was bloody living! Why would you want to be anywhere else?

Within days we spotted big numbers of brumbies. Now it was time to gather a decent herd. With the help of the local Indigenous people, we built holding yards partly into the creek, so once caught and yarded, the brumbies could get to water and feed. Then it was time for the real hard yakka.

Day after day, we galloped flat out as we sorted the wild horses into smaller groups of around twenty or so, then herded them into the holding yards by evening. After a day of hard riding, it wasn't only the saddle area that copped a caning. We all suffered sore and dried-up throats from the constant yelling and aching limbs from cracking whips and straining to stay in the saddle of a madly galloping horse that seemed determined to unseat you at every twist and turn. It was as if your own horse was trying to bloody kill you. If you didn't keep your wits about you, these bastard brumbies would be all over you, kicking, biting, snapping and trying to take a piece out of you.

In a lot of western films, a rider will be sitting down in the saddle of a galloping horse. But a horse can't gallop flat-out like that for any great distance. It'd drop dead from bloody exhaustion, while leaving the rider's rear-end red raw from the constant thumping. A good Aussie bushman can sit on a horse for days on end, letting the horse amble along at its own pace, occasionally cantering after a stray. If the need arises, the rider can push his horse up to a full-throttle gallop, but only if he stands up in the stirrups with his rump well clear of the saddle, just like the jockeys at the races.

As we filled the yards over the next few weeks, we found that the younger brumbies weren't quite so skittish. Often, we rode them straight away to help in the roundups. Bloody good horses, they were. By leaving out the older, wilder mongrels, we found the work was starting to go smoothly, and we could herd the animals along at a slow but steady walk.

Our plan was to leave three of our men, along with a fair number of the Indigenous people and their families, at the Callabonna Creek camp to keep rounding up horses while we headed off with the first group. Those staying put would continue to gentle the brumbies and get them used to the humans, so they'd be ready for the long trek to the port.

One morning, at the crack of dawn, we headed off on the first leg of what was to be the hardest yakka I had ever done. The other two men and

I moved out with six of the Indigenous people and a herd of more than 200 brumbies, bound for Port Augusta. Our plan was to set up a few camps and large holding yards along the way, depending on the terrain and how far we managed to push the brumbies each day.

Keeping the mob in a bunch didn't stop some breakaways, so by camp time, around mid-afternoon each day, both the brumbies and riders were pretty well buggered. Our biggest problem then was stopping any of the bastards from wandering off during the night. With each passing day, the brumbies settled down. And, thanks to our Indigenous guides, we only had a few dry camps. These fellas seemed to know exactly where to find water and where to herd the horses, even when they hadn't been in that part of the country before.

We would often see a guide standing rigid on one leg, with the other foot resting on it, while gazing into space without a sound. Then he would come to me, pointing, saying, 'We go that way, boss. It's better.' And he was always right.

After a couple of weeks we came across a huge muddy area. It was a bit salty, like bore water, and was an offshoot from Lake Frome. It was an ideal area to start breaking in the brumbies. It was also a good base as it was halfway to the coast.

We were busy at it when a bunch of men came riding up from a homestead, apparently only a few miles from us. The manager, who'd heard about our big herd, had a welcome ready for us at his spacious home. He insisted we all spend a few days with him and his family while his station hands looked after the brumbies. Beaut! Just what we needed. We couldn't remember how long it had been since we'd last shaved. We must have stunk to high heaven. Our clothes and boots were in tatters. A more ragged bunch of men you were never likely to meet! Hot baths, a proper bed with clean sheets and a good feed left us all in a state of shock. It was a bitch that we couldn't stay as long as we'd have liked, but time was against us, and three of our men were still back of beyond.

Our hosts, Dave and Lilly McGuire, were from the old school of back country people – real salt-of-the-earth sorts. Dave had worked on the property since he was a kid. Both the lake and homestead were named after Edward Frome, an explorer who mapped the area in 1843.

After our all-too-short break and catching up on the war news, we returned to our Lake Frome base to carry on breaking the horses to saddle.

Now, the fastest way to break a horse in is to throw on a saddle and blindfold, then jump on board, whip the blindfold off and ride until the horse accepts that you are not going to get off. In theory that would work if you only had to do it to a few horses. But for a mob of 200 wild horses, plus another 800 on the way, forget it. I had guaranteed the army 1000 head of saddled horses, yet here we were with only a handful and plenty of work to do.

A lot of men from the Frome station spent time with us, all trying their hand as they believed they were the better horsemen. Well, they all walked away on bowed legs, very sore in the nether regions. At this point, my mates and I feared we may have bitten off more than we could chew. It was only the thought of returning home with our tails between our legs that stopped us from giving it all away. I reckoned I would have been lucky if I even had a wife and kids to go back to. Would they even recognise me? Even with the hot bath at the homestead, I was still a dirty bloody stinking swagman in rags. I didn't even recognise myself. Was all this worth it? I couldn't see how we could break in so many wild horses and deliver on time, if at all. But there had to be a way.

'Think, Bibby,' I told myself. 'Put your bloody head down and think, you bastard.' Hope against hope, I told myself there was always a way out of every problem. I let my mind wander. Is a horse frightened of humans? No. Does it worry a horse to have a weight on its back? Not really. Will it be guided by humans? Yes, we'd already proved that by herding and breaking in over 200 head of wild horses by curbing their wild energy simply and swiftly.

Solution! We'd ride the bastards in the thick mud of the lake! The gluggy ground would bog the beasts down and stop them jumping. If they couldn't jump, they couldn't buck and if they couldn't buck, we could control them. So simple.

Over the next two weeks of gut-busting work, we saddled and rode the entire herd in a mud pit near the lake. One after the other, we got these brumbies to accept that the saddle and the riders were not going to hurt them. We soon had the whole mob well in hand.

I sent two men back to meet up with the others, who would have another 200 brumbies on the way down. I could only do this because the station manager offered me as much assistance as I would need. He said it was to help win the war. Luck was on our side.

Over the months that followed, we finally delivered just near a thousand of the now 'broken in' brumbies to Port Augusta and could all head back home by train with a pocket full of the good stuff. It had been no bloody picnic, I can tell you. But the cash felt good, as did the thought that those brumbies were going to help our fellas overseas. Those horses were a tough breed, and definitely up for it. Any Light Horseman riding one was going to be one hell of a lucky bastard.

It was a long trip by train from the port all the way to Brisbane. But at last, I was home, arriving early in July. Christ, it was great to see Florence and the kids. They were pretty damn excited.

Even though I had my hard-earned dough, I still felt I had to work. That was me. I couldn't sit on my arse, unless it was in a saddle. I was a bloody horseman. No way was I going belly up to a bloody counter, waiting on stupid bastards to hand me a white feather. It was time to join my brothers. In late July 1916, I joined the armed services, ready to fight for my country.

But on my first day of training, I wondered why I'd bothered. First off, some nincompoop officer tried to tell me how to ride a horse, then another was telling me how to shoot a rifle. Christ almighty; I could shoot the eye out of a needle! Then they wanted me marching. What for? I was a horseman, I told them. In no uncertain terms. Next thing I knew I was up before the sergeant. He wanted to know why I was so unruly and why I refused to take orders. I lowered my head and said: 'Sir, my wife is an alcoholic and I am terribly afraid she may do damage to our little kids. Please, sir, can I go home and care for them?' I was discharged just three months later, on 18 October 1916. It was in their best bloody interests! The way I had been feeling, it wasn't just the enemy that was going to get a bullet to the head from my rifle!

When laughingly I told Florence why I was discharged, for the first time in her life she went off her face, screaming at me. 'I have never hurt my kids in my life! How dare you!' She slapped me hard. 'My father owned a pub, but I've never touched a drink in my life!' Slap!

It took lots of cuddles before she eventually forgave me. Sheilas.

Chapter 5

Up and Running Again

1916–1920s

Needing a steady earner close to home, while still missing his old life in the circus, Bert hit upon a compromise of sorts. He would go into business as a 'while-you-wait' photographer, working at carnivals or simply on street corners.

The camera, a large box-like contraption mounted on tripod legs, allowed the operator to develop and print each photo in less than five minutes. Through the later war years, this wonderful machine proved popular with young servicemen and their girlfriends. Many of these souvenir photos were no doubt carried off to war in servicemen's pockets, giving the soldiers a little hope to cling to amid the bloodshed.

With the war finally ended in 1918, Bert sought out his brothers, hoping they had returned safely and been demobbed. He found Ted at the Heidelberg Repatriation Centre in Melbourne. He was suffering from acute bronchitis, brought on by mustard gas. Of John, there was no word. (Years later, John was found to have died in 1919 in Melbourne. Nobody knows why or how, but a pub fight was a safe bet. When Ted was finally released from the Heidelberg hospital, he moved into a small apartment, where he lived out the rest of his life. He never married and died at the age of seventy-three, in 1960.)

Sadly, many ex-servicemen found themselves on the streets after the war, drifting from town to town. This was the era of the swagman, begging for work and collecting food coupons from the local police station. A number of these returned solders looked to showgrounds and circus lots for any type of work, just to be able to eat. Starting as roustabouts, many became showmen in their own right, running games and developing sideshows. Some became boxing-tent fighters.

Having effectively declared himself unfit for the army, my father Bert now found himself among the ranks of these downtrodden diggers. Like many of these returned soldiers, he was drawn to the show life, the life he knew best anyway. He soon began to work exclusively in sideshow alley, operating his photo service out of a canvas stall. A painted banner above the doorway – The Hollywood Studio – gave more class to his product and enticed the general public in a more refined manner than shouting from a street corner.

But in these first few years following the war, there was little money coming in and plenty going out. Bert was forced to sell the house. Once again, the family was on the road. Florence and the two children would have to make do with beds built into an ex-military truck, which Bert had bought from the army surplus yards. It was pretty rough and ready, but it was no worse than what the other show people had.

Even by Florence's account, it wasn't all doom and gloom. Though it was Bert who revelled the most in the close camaraderie of the show people, this time Florence too, who had often experienced being alone with her young kids in Tasmania and Brisbane, found this communal life had its appeal. And more importantly, this way she could be with her husband. Once the evening meal was over, it was normal to throw a log or two on the fire as an invitation for families to gather around for an hour or two of singing and storytelling. There was many a wonderful evening round the campfire for the couple's fast-growing kids, listening to Bert's many stories.

Aside from photography during these lean years, Bert would often play less refined games of chance, like two-up, at the public drinking bars. Two-up was Australia's true-blue national pastime. Often played in pubs, it was popular with swaggies and servicemen alike as it only needed two pennies and a kip – a small flat piece of wood for the pennies to be placed on.

How to Play Two-Up

Also known as swy, two-up was Australia's true-blue national pastime, just as it was Bert Bibby's. Many a showman played two-up while on a break or around the campfire at night. Often played in pubs, the game was popular with swaggies and servicemen alike as it only needed two pennies and a kip – a small flat piece of wood for the pennies to be placed on. Today it is only legal to play two-up in Australia on Anzac Day.

Like all great pastimes, the game has its own lingo:

Boxer – game owner who runs the game and betting and doesn't place his own bet

Ringie – supervisor in the ring

Kip – flat board used to throw the coins

Spinner – player who tosses the pennies

Sling – tip given to the boxer.

During the build-up to the game, there is a lot of shouting as the bets are laid. When the boxer is sure that all bets have been placed, the ringie will call in the spinner. The ringie walks to the centre of the ring, which is surrounded by the punters, who call out phrases like 'tennahead' (meaning ten dollars on both coins landing on heads). Nobody can question the ringie; his decision is final.

With the ringie's call of 'Come in, spinner!', the spinner uses the kip to flip the two coins, tail-side up, into the air. All eyes are on the spinning coins, with the ringie making sure that the coins are tossed at least three metres high.

As the coins land on the ground within the circle, the shout will go up, 'It's heads; it's a pair of heads!' or 'It's a pair of tails!' Heads means the spinner wins, tails the spinner loses. One of each is odds, which means the coins must continue to be tossed until there's a result. If you're the spinner and the result is tails, the ringie will pass the kip on to the next player.

But betting games weren't the only way Bert earned a quid at the pub. There was also money to be made with his fists. In whatever town pub he was in, Bert would size up a mouthy local and challenge him to a fight, bare knuckle. Sometimes he'd even have a pre-punch-up drink with his adversary, because a man with a belly full of beer is easy to beat. Bert would just put the beer up to his mouth and pretend to swallow it. He was a tricky blighter! By organising the bets himself, he won a lot of money and never lost a fight. Bert's fighting skills were sometimes his salvation monetarily, but later they were to be a curse.

In between fights, Bert was spending more time at the pubs, or around the fire late at night, drinking with his mates. His frequent visits to the pub meant Florence was pining again for home in New Zealand.

By 1927, with their two children at the end of their teen years, Florence managed to talk Bert into shifting the family 'home' to New Zealand. There, they settled into the agricultural show run, with Bert continuing his photography stall. This proved to be a good move, as many Maori people had never seen a while-you-wait camera and queued up for photos that specifically showed up their tribal tattoos.

While Bert was doing well financially, the kids were growing up fast. Seventeen-year-old son Frank was flirting with the best of them, and daughter Edna at eighteen was being courted by an older man, Arthur Gerrand. The owner of a large number of riding devices and games in a well-established travelling carnival, Arthur was totally smitten with beautiful Edna. Within a few months he had convinced her to become his wife.

But next came some bad news. Florence, who'd been feeling unwell, was found to be suffering from an incurable cancerous growth. It ultimately took her life, in March 1928. She was only thirty-four. It seemed Bert had returned to his place of birth only to bury his wife.

In his grief, Bert found New Zealand had lost its appeal. With Edna married off, he turned to Frank with a new plan. Father and son would return to Australia to try their luck as showmen. The timing seemed right, on the surface at least.

In Australia, Bert and Frank found that the travelling show people had finally found a way to better co-ordinate the helter-skelter nature of the carnival business. With the formation of showmen's guilds, they could at last work hand in hand with the various agricultural shows. It wasn't the first time this had been attempted. Before the war, the Showmen's Association was formed in 1909 on the old showgrounds in Orange, New South Wales. My father had been one of the founding members. Unfortunately, it didn't last long. With members invariably out of town, it was difficult to put a quorum together, so the association gradually faded away.

The second Showmen's Association was formed a few years later at Bob Parker's 'Coney Drome', an indoor carnival set up during

Easter each year at the bottom end of Pitt Street, Sydney. It also was disbanded after a very brief run. Then, in 1927, the Showmen's Guild of Australasia (SGA) was formed in Warton's sideshow tent on the Sydney showgrounds following the Royal Easter Show. This guild covered all New South Wales, Queensland and the Northern Territory (with my father becoming a proud member for more than fifty years). The Victorian Showman's Guild and others followed on, all working as a united band of people around Australia to assist each other if and when the need should arise. That was the idea, anyway. It didn't always work out as intended, as we were to find out later.

One of the first things the Showman's Guild did was to allocate each showman a permanent space at the various annual agricultural shows. On this space, the showman would then operate his sideshow equipment. An agreed rental was collected by the guild from each showman, on a per-foot frontage basis. The guild then paid the collected money to the show society of that town. This ensured all showmen got a 'piece of the pie' and each knew well in advance just how much space he had available at each show.

Over time, these spaces could be handed down from showman father to showman son, generation to generation. Such spaces could also be swapped with other guild members to improve their sites, or gifted on retirement. This still goes on today, with the guild being notified and records kept by the various showman guilds in each state.

With the establishment of the guild system in 1927, so began a new era for sideshow entertainers, who had endured almost unspeakable hardships over the years. The horse and wagons were now a thing of the past. A new phase had begun for the industry. The circus and show folk were no longer the rough-and-ready families who had once wandered all over the land, living in tents and cooking on open campfires. They now had motorised vehicles, and many show families were living in trailered caravans. Sideshow alley had a different look too, with mechanically driven riding devices along with painted banners and pictorials on the sideshows. A showman owned and maintained his own equipment and was totally independent, even though he often worked with others as a group. From the 1900s right through to the 1970s, it was rare for one showman to operate both rides and stalls or sideshows and food vans.

During these years, the old megaphone would become defunct and a new microphone with huge horn speakers would come into vogue. This would be a boon to all sideshow people. Quite a few of the showgrounds now had electricity available for the showmen to use. Much was changing.

For Bert and Frank, the signs were good. But dark clouds were again forming far from Australian shores. The Great Depression was about to hit hard worldwide. If Bert thought his run of misfortune was over, he was mistaken.

Chapter 6

Love Is in the Air

Early–mid 1930s

Out of the 1920s and into the tumultuous 1930s, Bert and Frank Bibby scraped their way through the Great Depression as a struggling sideshow team. They earned a living the best way they could over these difficult few years, mostly with the while-you-wait photos. Times were tough, but the general public seemed to be able to come up with a few bob to play on the games and rides. And on one particular day, for Bert, things were really looking up.

'Strike a light. What a beauty!' Bert had just spied a gorgeous young lady in the line-up of beauties at Dolly Baker's burlesque show. He'd always had an eye for the pretty girls. And, oh boy, was this filly lovely, with her long, fair hair and her barely-there shorts and wrap-around top. He was pretty sure she blushed when his gaze lingered on her.

The dancer's name was Violet. And, given her history, it was no wonder the older, and still handsome, Bert caught her attention. Violet's husband had gone off to war in India, leaving her with two young children. To make a quid, Violet had become a burlesque dancer. What else was a girl to do? In the end, unable to care for her children, she adopted them out. Not an easy decision for any mother.

Now, ol' Dolly Baker was very protective of her girls. She'd belt any bloke who tried to get his hands on a dancer. Bert must have sweet-talked Dolly no end just to meet this girl, let alone get her in the family way, at the age of 50! Bert and Violet officially became partners in late 1934. They were unable to marry as she was still technically married. It was probably just as well that Violet's husband was missing in action, otherwise Bert might have been!

Young Frank had likewise fallen for a very pretty girl by the name of Mavis Rogan, sister to the popular Australian showman Alan Barton (Rogan was Alan's family name). With Frank engaged and Violet now pregnant, the Bibby men needed money more than ever.

Bert decided to get back into the fight game, sensing there was a small fortune to be made. Though he was getting on in years, Bert was still in good shape. With Frank as his assistant, father and son would head for far north Queensland to take on the young cane cutters, who Bert figured were flush with cash and spoiling for a bit of bare-knuckle action. Planning to be gone for twelve weeks at most, Bert and Frank looked forward to making enough dough to settle down with their 'brides'.

While Bert installed Violet in a rented house in Bowen Hills, close to the Brisbane showgrounds, Frank travelled north by rail to the sugarcane towns of Bundaberg and beyond. The young fella's job was to locate the resident bully in each of these places. (From Bert's experience, there was a fight-happy bruiser to be found in every town.) He would then organise a date for a bare-knuckle fight in a local pub. The publican was to gather all the bets and hold the betting purse until after the fight, whereupon the money would be paid to the winner, less an agreed percentage for the publican.

It all went to plan at first, with Bert holding his own in each pub fight up the coast. As the money rolled in, they stashed it away for their respective, rosy futures. They were on track to be back in Brisbane in time for the birth of Violet's first baby to Bert.

Arriving in Bowen for the last fight on the agenda, they were resting up in their hotel room when Frank mentioned to his dad that he wasn't feeling well. He'd been suffering with stomach cramps for some time.

'You'll be right, mate,' Bert said. 'It's only a bellyache. You can rest up on the train home.' The show had to go on.

An area had been cleared in the backyard of Bowen's Railway Hotel. A huge crowd had gathered for the evening fight, with everyone vying for the best spot. The hulking young local who Bert was to take on was not only a bully, he was also a braggart whose brother was the town's local police sergeant. Threats had been made. Bert was warned that if he won, he wouldn't get out of town in one piece. The big bully also had a team of local yokels to back him up.

As the crowd bayed for blood, the publican showed off a betting purse brimming with money. Then the bell clanged. The fight was on. The local lad came at Bert in a flurry, his arms flying like windmills. His mates were yelling and cheering him on. Bang. Crash. Wallop. He was everywhere at once. Bert was dodging and ducking to keep out of his way. *Let the big ox wear himself out*, he thought.

Round followed round of bareknuckle punches. The spectators were getting increasingly rowdy as their man huffed and puffed and started to run out of steam. At the fifth-round break, a couple of louts started throwing stones at Bert as he rested in his corner.

'Righto, get ready to collect,' Bert told Frank. 'It's time to get out of here.'

As the bell clanged for the sixth round, Bert sprang from his corner with fists flying. Within a minute, it was all over. The local was down and out for the count, in front of a shocked audience. Across the way, a train was just pulling into Bowen station. Bert and Frank had planned ahead. Wherever possible, they had arranged for the fights to take place in pubs nearest a train station. Before each stoush, Bert made sure to check the railway timetable in case he and Frank had to make a dash for it. This was most certainly one of those occasions. With the train about to leave the station, Bert and Frank snatched up their belongings and bolted. They could hear the local boys swearing and searching for them back in the pub. Bert reached the train just as it began to gather speed. Jumping onto the open veranda at the rear, he reached back to help his son aboard.

Frank was running flat out then, suddenly, he was gone. Without a thought, Bert leaped off the moving train. Frank was screaming in pain somewhere in the dark. He soon found that Frank had fallen into a cinder pit, a 6-foot-deep trench used to store ash from a coal train's fire box.

By the time help arrived and they got Frank to the local hospital, it was too late. His appendix had burst. While enduring the pain that day, peritonitis had set in. By morning he was gone. Francis 'Frank' Albert Bibby died on 2 July 1935 and was buried in Bowen General Cemetery, in the same town he was running for his life from.

Frank went to his grave aged just twenty-three, never knowing he was to become a father. His son, Kevin, was born seven months later.

Bert was gutted by Frank's death. He blamed himself for encouraging his son to push through his cramps and pain for that one last fight. Just so the show could go on.

When Violet gave birth to a little girl on 25 August 1935, Bert named his new daughter Francis Teresa Bibby, in honour of his lost son. And he took up the bottle.

As Bert spent more and more time with his cronies in pubs and bars, money grew very tight. Violet copped the brunt of his uncontrolled temper. Yet before long she was once again pregnant. And they were on the road again, following the show route.

In September of that year, Bert, Violet and baby Francis were driving near Innisfail on the northern show run when Bert's bomb of a truck got stuck in a creek. A local farmer, Jim Benson, brought in two of his most powerful dray horses, but even they couldn't move the truck. It was bogged to the axles. To cap it all off, Violet started going into labour. What the bloody hell to do? The farmer's wife, a mother of six, immediately took over. She sent her husband with baby Francis to the farmhouse, to be cared for by her older children. He was then to bring back the dray (an open-top wagon) to transport Violet. The men spread a bale of hay in the tray, covering it with some canvas so that Violet could lie on it in some semblance of comfort. With Mrs Benson assisting Violet on her makeshift bed as the men drove the wagon, they headed for the Innisfail hospital, three miles away.

They never quite made it. The baby was born not far from the hospital gates. My charming father's heartfelt response was said to be: 'Not another bloody sheila.'

That bloody sheila was me. Enter, Norma. Just Norma, no middle name. The story goes that I was the last show child in Australia born in the back of a wagon.

Chapter 7

My Earliest Memories

1936–1938

'Whoa, stop ya mongrel!' My father was yelling at his old rattletrap of a truck. He pulled back on the steering wheel with his feet clamped to the floor.

This was one of my earliest recollections of Bert. He always seemed to drive angrily. Still, I didn't feel nervous. I never felt nervous back in these early days of my life.

Like the other show people we travelled with, we lived out of a tent. The roads we traversed were little more than bush tracks between towns. There were few bridges spanning the waterways, so we moved in groups, often camping at river crossings where we all helped each other. I distinctly remember Mum driving the truck through fast-flowing streams, while Dad hoisted me on his shoulders and carried me across.

The Show Trains

Before the 1930s, the biggest bugbear facing the show people travelling the Queensland run on the east coast was the 'road to hell' – the Bruce Highway. On the nearly always wet and muddy road, a truck would inevitably go one way while the van or trailer it was towing went the other. Slipping and sliding their way from Brisbane to Cairns and back, show people often found that all that was left of their beautiful home was the undercarriage.

At the finish of each show the showmen would rush to pack to be among the first trucks to leave the showgrounds. Nobody wanted to end up behind the semis with their huge loads of monster rides, or get caught by the worst of the wet season. A solution was needed!

By the early 1930s, Wirth's Circus had their own train system up and running to avoid the notorious Bruce Highway. Keen for all show people to travel this way, the president of the Showmen's Guild visited Wirth's with an idea in mind. After many conferences with the Queensland Railways, a joint undertaking was secured between our Showmen's Guild and the Queensland Railways, with the showmen making their bookings through the Guild at special rates for Guild members. A delegation of showmen was then appointed to control all the loading and unloading at each town for the entire run, starting from Brisbane with stopovers at each town on the way to Cairns.

In May 1936, the very first of these Showmen's Trains left Clapham Junction, Brisbane, heading right through to Cairns in the far north of Queensland, just over 1700 kilometres. The first stop was Gympie, with the train stopping at all large and small towns along the coast where an agricultural show was being held. From Cairns it was a non-stop return run direct to Brisbane for the annual Brisbane Royal Agricultural Show.

From that first trial run, the number of trains grew to seven, with the loading and unloading being carried out by the show people themselves. The trains operated for the next twenty-seven years (except for a couple of years during World War II).

As these special trains travelled slowly through the smaller towns, the shout would go out, 'The show people are here!' Hundreds of men, women and children would line the railway lines, shouting and waving.

The excitement was contagious. With the show train's arrival, irrespective of what hour of the day or night it was, the crowds would be there. Little did they know all the work that went into getting on that train in time after show closing time each day. Despite exhaustion from setting up and working the show, the show folk had to do the pull-down and then make a mad dash to the loading ramps at the station to get there by 10pm. If you weren't on time for your place in the queue, you went to the end of the line, and there you stayed for the rest of the trip north. Everything had to be precisely on time, or you missed out.

The loading of the first division of the train would usually take place about 5.30pm, once the people were leaving the grounds on the final day of the show. By 7.30pm, the first division was on its way to the next town. The loading continued right through the night until the last of the mechanical rides were loaded and all five trains were on their way, including the three circus/vaudeville trains.

When the train reached its show town, there was no time to lose – everything had to be ready to work in a matter of hours. With each showman's space already allotted on the showgrounds by the delegates, many showmen would work late into the night to set up on their given site. After a brief nap they would then appear, sparkly eyed and bushy-tailed, ready to work on show day.

The show trains covered the north Queensland coastal run of agricultural shows until the cost of rail travel grew too much, and many of the show people once again took to the road in the early- to mid-60s.

From an early age, I was often allowed to sit around the campfires with the adults. I would listen to yarns or songs played by accordionist Sis Bourke, or old Johnny Foster on his banjo. It was amazing when I think back just how many showfolk had beautiful voices and were musically inclined.

My father was in his best form on nights like this. Beside the fire, with a beer or a tin cup of hot tea, he would regale one and all with his many tales. That's how I learnt much of the history for this book. I know I am similar to my father in quite a few ways: appearance, mannerisms, yarn-spinning and our bloody stubbornness. (Of course, I was much prettier.)

Through these years, one of my parents' biggest concerns was whether we had enough fuel to get to the next town. There was also the problem of toilets, not only for the travelling show people but also for the public who attended the agricultural shows. The search for a decent thunderbox, bull-pit, dunny, shithouse, long-drop, bog-hole or brasco (yes, they had many names) was endless. A familiar sight at a show was the long queue to use the outhouse. Meantime, the very upmarket shows provided loos in the form of a container of lime and a bucket of sawdust, complete with a goodly supply of cut-up newspaper, in lieu of toilet rolls.

One time, when we were preparing for a show at Mount Gravatt in Brisbane, it was the dunnies that provided the entertainment. The show society had supplied two floorless, timber toilets, which had been set down under a large gum tree. When nobody was looking, a couple of showie scallywags, 'Snooky' Godfrey and 'Sparrow' Baker, rigged up the gents' toilet for some fun and games.

The next day, Sparrow's father, a huge bloke by the name of Sonny, made his way to the toilet. Sonny was comfortably ensconced on the throne, reading his newspaper, when suddenly – whoosh – the cubicle was hoisted high up into the gum tree. Poor old Sonny was left sitting there in all his glory, pants around his ankles, to the uncontrollable laughter of those around. Yep, these showies knew how to have a bit of fun.

Another day, a group of young show people had a few too many drinks at a pub and ended up being carted off to the lock-up to sober up. The attending policeman asked for names to enter into the daily ledger.

'I'm Stanley Green, and he's my brother Headley Green,' Stanley answered.

The officer pointed to the next bloke.

'I'm Hoppy Pink.'

The next man said, 'I'm Darcy Brown.'

'Oh, we're going to be smart-arses, are we?' the copper said. 'I suppose your name is Black or White!'

'No sir,' answered the last man, drawing himself up with as much dignity as possible. 'My name is Joseph Percival Blow. But I am better known as "Joe Blow" or "Blow-off".'

I cannot repeat what the policeman had to say.

The fact is that every word of this story is true. Without a doubt, truth is stranger than fiction.

I knew very early on that show day was a big event in all Australian towns. Schoolchildren got a day off for the main show day, and farming families got dolled up to come into town and spend a few bob on the games and see the latest farming machinery. Much has changed over the years, but in many ways, it's the same today.

For the general public, 'the Show' was always a rare and special event. But for us showies, it felt like it was every day. We breathed and moved as a group. I grew up feeling connected with everybody around me in our community. We all felt that. It was something the locals might have found hard to understand. We showies had a true sense of belonging, by banding together. Some of the travelling show people were from circus families, others from vaudeville entertainment and some from the carnivals, rodeos and agricultural shows. Most of the circuses had carnivals on the outside of their huge marquees, which operated before and during interval. Some even travelled the rodeo circuit. All the businesses and families overlapped like a giant puzzle. Every man, woman and child was prepared to work long hours in all kinds of weather so that the show could go on. It wasn't just a cliché. The show people were, and still are, survivors. There was no room for complainers or hypochondriacs in the outdoor entertainment industry. If you were ill you went to hospital, got treated and then went back to work.

Still, it was something of a miracle that these showmen stared down the dark days of the 1930s, let alone the spectre of another bloody world war. But survive we did. And the money flowed both ways. While the occasional grumpy local would say, 'You lot just come here to take our money and then leave,' most people realised we were good for business. Wherever we went, we brought a boom for shopkeepers and the like. While we were setting up our equipment, these traders would drop by to collect and deliver orders. Back in those days, very few show people owned a car, so a trip to town would mean a lot of walking. That the traders came to us was a welcome bonus.

I remember their voices calling out their wares …

The butcher: 'Take your order now!'

The greengrocer: 'Fresh fruit and vegies cheap at half price!'

The drycleaner: 'Back tomorrow, all nice and clean!'

The grocer: 'Take your order now. Delivery this arvo!'

And let's not forget the milko and the baker. In each town we stopped in, we lived for the fresh milk and bread. Yum!

When these locals came calling, my mother and the other show women would stop whatever they were doing – hanging washing, cleaning the caravans, cooking, practising their acts, tidying the tents or sewing costumes – to hurry and buy supplies.

For me, seeing the bags of sugar being delivered was always a special occasion. For one thing, it meant fairy floss. As a youngster, I'd watch the fluffy pink clouds being spun in a huge bowl by Bill McDonald, who'd usually pass me a free scoop on a slip of paper. Bill's fairy floss machine was manually operated, with the sugar poured into the spindle at the top. The sugar was heated by a primus stove underneath and then the whole spindle was set spinning, throwing the fairy floss into the catching bowl, where it would be scooped onto paper and sold for one penny a serve. The cellophane bags were first introduced in 1952, by Bill, most likely at the Sydney Royal Easter Show.

The first patent for a 'cotton candy' machine was granted to Americans John Wharton and William Morrison in 1897. When the sugary treat was introduced in Australia, a young sideshow operator, who called himself Major Wilson, felt that the name 'cotton candy' would make people think the stuff was actually made of cotton wool. He suggested that it be changed to 'fairy floss', which was in fact the name it was first given at the St Louis World's Fair in 1904.

I also remember well watching fresh apples being skewered on a stick then dipped into a huge vat of boiling hot toffee. Ah, the crunch of the apple smothered in bright red toffee. And yet I don't think I ever went to the dentist when I was a kid. It's a wonder, with the amount of toffee apples and fairy floss I ate!

Another favourite show food of mine was waffles filled with fresh cream. Bill Green and his wife – better known as 'Pop' and 'Mater' – came into the show business at the peak of the Great Depression with a few games and kiddies' rides. But before long they switched to food, finding the sweet spot with their freshly-made waffles. No matter how hot the weather, Pop and Mater's mob would spend hour after hour standing before a row of griddle irons, pouring the batter mix. They rolled the red-hot waffles into cylinders, ready to fill to the brim with luscious cream when cooled. I too spent many an hour rolling the waffles into paper sleeves, stacking hundreds of them into specially made containers, ready for showtime.

As the years went by, the waffle griddles weren't the only thing heating up. The public were wanting more flesh. And so came the era of the girlie shows, sometimes called 'the striptease' or 'the leg and belly show'. The girls themselves were called 'stripteasers'.

One of the most notable and long-lasting operators (from mid-1930s to 1970s) was Marie 'Ma' Short. Marie ran several variety sideshows and had a reputation for putting a complete sideshow together overnight. In her later years, the charismatic seventy-year-old Ma could still be found spruiking shows like 'Judy the Judo Girl'. Hitching her skirt to flash a bit of chubby leg, she would stand on her line-up board in front of her painted banners, touting into her microphone.

'Come on, boys. It's time to see a beauty – Judy the Judo girl! But wait, first let's see which one of you can manage to plant a kiss on lovely Judy's ruby red lips within ten seconds, for a five-pound note!'

The young men all lined up, hopeful to have a go. Alas, very few ever won. Judy's martial arts skills would keep them at bay. Most men who got close ended up smeared with bright red lipstick. I always found this hilarious.

Chapter 8

Mischief and Survival

1930s–1945

During the 1930s, our family settled in Lismore, New South Wales, with Dad doing shift work at the railyards. The agricultural shows right around Australia had started to close down as World War II was looming. Rations on fuel had already started, which meant the carnivals were also disbanding. This time, Mum had to enter the workforce too to help put food on the table. But what to do with us girls? Oh, no problem – she could take us with her. Well, it turned out that *was* a problem.

Our mum had befriended a lady named Mrs Macintyre, who was the head housekeeper at Lismore's St Mary's Convent. She managed to find Mum some work as a cleaner at the convent, for a few hours each day. Mrs Macintyre also said Mum could bring us girls along. We could play with her seven-year-old son, Max.

Max had curly jet-black hair and was small for his age. But he made up for that with his energy. This boy was a mischief-maker … like me, as it turned out. We became good mates and went everywhere together. We got into all sorts of strife, with the result that the long-suffering nuns quite often separated us by locking me in with a group of pre-schoolers.

The pre-schoolers were confined to a circular building called 'The Rex'. With windows all around, it was a bit like an enclosed gazebo – weatherproof and perfect for this purpose. One day, I was peering out of a window of The Rex, wishing I was mucking about with Max, when flames leapt up the building outside. Everyone screamed, including the nuns, and we were all rushed outside. The gardener came and managed to extinguish the fire with a bucket of water. What had happened?

Well, Max, in a fit of temper because he wasn't allowed to play with me, had piled a heap of dry brush up against the wall of the Rex and set fire to it. The damage was minimal, but my mother was severely chastised by the nuns for having an unruly daughter. Apparently, I had tempted little Max into this mischievous act. Go figure.

With that, our stay in Lismore came to an end. We headed south to Tamworth, with my father picking up work wherever possible. We stayed put for some time, as once again my mother was expecting and was ill throughout her pregnancy. In our business, the babies were born at whichever town we happened to be in. Likewise, our people were buried all over Australia. My new baby sister was born on New Year's Day, 1939. She lived only fifteen minutes and was never named. She was buried in Tamworth. Mum was devastated.

Following the funeral, my sister and I spent a lot of time with Mum. The loss of her baby had hit her hard. Dad didn't seem to know what to do. Eventually he decided things would be better in Melbourne, where some of Mum's friends were now living. So that's where we headed.

Easier said than done. With war and conscription looming, all non-essential travel by road, train or even foot was banned. Fuel coupons and travel passes had to be obtained from the army. So Dad contacted a friend who had connections to the Painters and Dockers' wharfie union in Melbourne. A job was available on the wharves, so we were able to travel.

Not so fortunate were the many showmen and circus families who had their vehicles confiscated by the armed forces, which immediately put many out of business with no hope of compensation. We were lucky our small truck was also our living quarters. Fitted out like a caravan with beds and cupboards, it couldn't be confiscated.

Once we arrived in Melbourne, Dad hatched a plan. He set up our camping truck in a yard near the Russell Street police station. After his shift work at the wharf, he ran games of two-up in the lane, with the coppers happy to turn a blind eye.

What a safe haven this laneway proved to be, with all the security possible provided by the boys in blue, whose back door opened onto the lane. The coppers would often pop their heads out and join in the ruckus as the coins were thrown into the air and punters cheered. They even placed a bet or two. There was no way these coppers were going to arrest old Bert Bibby for playing two-up in their own backyard.

But one day a constable came running. 'Bibby, you're about to get raided. Run!' A new sergeant at the station had decided it was time to clean up this backyard situation, and make a name for himself. My quick-thinking father grabbed the loot and dived for cover in the safest place he knew, well out of sight. Then uniformed police, led by the sergeant, came rushing in to break up the game. 'Put your hands up!' The police were yelling and waving their batons.

The coppers raced after the gamblers as they clambered over fences and down the alley. Once the hue and cry had settled down, my dad emerged from his hidey hole – the police station! He tipped his hat to the sergeant as he calmly strolled out the front door.

As Dad later stated, 'It was the perfect place to hide!'

My own mischief-making continued in Melbourne too. Even as a five-year-old, I ran wild, which often ended up in a belting. Meanwhile, my more conservative sister took on the full-time job of looking after our mother.

In today's world, our poor mother would have been diagnosed with postnatal depression and anxiety. She spent hours in tears, often threatening to harm herself as she felt she was to blame for her baby's death. That she had adopted out her first two babies must have also played on her mind. People didn't talk about that stuff in those days. Maybe she felt guilty at losing not just one baby but three! At a loss for a solution, Dad got crankier and more stressed by the day, often hitting the bottle.

My mother's misery and my father's mood weighed heavily on me. Though I was only five years old, I often escaped to see my ailing Uncle Ted in his flat, which was only a short walk from St Patrick's Cathedral in East Melbourne. I know it seems strange that a five-year-old could roam the busy streets of a major city like Melbourne, but I was a tough little bugger. I believe that showed in my attitude of having no fear of anything or anyone.

I'd also take off and visit Wirth's Olympia Circus by the Yarra River. I remember the last time I did this. I took off from Russell Street, sneaking out while Dad was at work and Mum was hiding in her room. I'd usually take the long walk to Flinders Street Railway Station, but this time I figured I'd be clever. As a tram stopped, I managed to sneak on beside a mother and children. I wiggled my way to the back exit and got off at the Flinders Street station. I was pretty chuffed about saving that one penny tram fare!

I walked over the river via Princes Bridge to St Kilda Road, where the circus, carnival and skating rink awaited. Getting food was no problem. I was one of the show kids, and everyone fed the show kids. These were my mates.

'Hey, Bluey,' I said, peering up at the old showie who ran the hot dog stand.

'Hey, Norma. Where's your dad?'

'Oh, he's at work today, so he sent me here to play. Mum's sick.'

Bluey nodded, a knowing look on his face, and handed me a hot dog.

I spent a good part of the day going around the stalls and

getting free rides. Just when I was thinking of getting another toffee apple, I heard a booming voice. 'Norma!'

Whoops. It was Dad. I was in for it. No point in running. He grabbed my hand and hauled me away, stony-faced. He didn't say another word until we were home. Then he lost it.

'Bloody kid! Always doing your own thing.' Wallop! He backhanded me across the face. I went flying across the kitchen from the force. It hurt, but I didn't cry. I never cried when he hit me. I gave him a hell of a steely stare. I might cry later in my bed, but I'd never let him see it.

Oh, how many backhanders I got from my dad over the years. Like many men from this era, he would let fly without a second thought, especially in response to my answering back during his angry outbursts. It was not unusual for me to sport a bruised eye.

My runaway routine was too much for Dad, especially as Mum's health took a turn for the worse. She had stopped crying but was fading away. She was a shell of a person. Deep in depression, she was finally hospitalised. At the same time, my sister and I were sent to the Convent of the Good Shepherd in nearby Abbotsford. We were to be incarcerated. Well, that's how it felt!

As Francis was six years old, she could go to school with the other convent kids, but I was still considered a bub. So, I had to spend my time with the bubs – silly little blighters who would cry for nothing at all. I wasn't a bub!

It seemed so unfair that we were locked up in this great mausoleum called a convent, with all these scary ladies in long black dresses, with beads instead of belts to hold up their skirts. No matter where I hid, these nuns would hunt me down. They were always chastising me and making me stand in a corner with my face to the wall, while telling me that God loved me. Why were they always punishing me? It couldn't have been because of the worms that mysteriously turned up in the dining room, or the lizard or frog that managed to get into the Mother Superior's office, could it?

I made half a dozen escape attempts, only to be caught on each occasion. To keep the increasingly furious nuns happy, my father would deliver a truckload of goods from the wharfs. Time and again, I was locked in the coal cellar to teach me a lesson. I think I finally got the message. I changed my ways and made sure to be good, so very good. Even so, we were returned to our father. I think I had worn out our welcome.

It was now 1941 and, once again, Dad was in a quandary. With shift work and two small kids to worry about, he had got word that my mother was being transferred to the hospital in St Arnaud, in north-west Victoria. Many patients were being moved from the large city hospitals as the beds were needed for injured returning soldiers.

After my mother was moved, Dad felt there was nothing to keep us in Victoria. With the help of his mates, and claiming that he had a sister in Brisbane to care for us kids, Dad successfully applied for an exemption from the war department to move to Queensland. There he could continue to work on the wharfs in the Port of Brisbane. Issued with special wartime railway passes, the three of us boarded the train at Spencer Street and headed north.

There were many soldiers on the train, most of them playing cards. My interest was piqued. I was pretty good at cards.

'Hello.' I'd smile sweetly at a group of soldiers.

'Hey, gorgeous,' they'd say, loving this little beauty with her golden hair. I could be as sweet as honey when I wanted.

'Can I play cards with you?'

'Sure! Pop up here between us. Are your hands big enough to hold the cards?'

Oh, please! I'd play these blokes at their own game, and play hard. I won lots of pennies to spend at the canteens at each stop. The diggers were onto me towards the end of the trip, as none of them would play me for money anymore.

By the time we arrived at Roma Street Station in Brisbane, I knew every inch of the trains we travelled on. I'd even badgered the drivers into helping them stoke the firebox with coal.

In Brisbane, we moved into a crowded boarding house, where some kind ladies looked after us girls while Dad worked at the docks. Everyone was always nice to us, probably because Dad was always giving them big parcels of fresh meat, tinned food and stuff, all 'confiscated' by Dad from the holding sheds at the docklands.

It was about this time that I realised I couldn't eat meat; every time I tried, I would get really sick and couldn't hold it down. I also noticed that it was no big deal, as meat was the hardest of all food to come by.

Our next move was quite the surprise – a zoo! Having suffered an injury when a load fell from one of the cranes at the wharf, Dad couldn't work the docks anymore. So he found a job as a caretaker at the abandoned Redcliffe Zoo, which included a cottage to live in.

The zoo had been closed for years; I don't know why – but it was a great place to play in. It didn't take long for Francis and me to mate up with some of the other kids who lived nearby. And what fun we had. The place was decrepit, but it was full of old buildings and empty cages to explore and hide in. We were in and out of everything.

In Redcliffe, my sister and I started primary school at a Catholic school. I did not take well to the classroom. What made it bearable was our little brown-and-white dog, Sally. She used to follow us to school, where she would hide until it was time to go home. She was a good little dog and would always – well, mostly – do as she was told. But on one particular day she wasn't happy, so she snuck inside and hid under our desk. I think she had a bellyache as she was making little whiney noises. With that, the nun spotted her. The outraged sister came rushing towards us, striking out at Sally with a cane. Francis tried to grab the dog, and over went the desk. Sally was now running madly in circles, trying to get out of this madhouse, while the kids yelled, screamed and cried. I was trying to grab the cane from the nun and getting belted across the shoulders for my trouble. Into this melee other nuns came rushing, finally managing to put a stop to the chaos. After this, I refused to go back to school, and both of us were finally expelled, to my father's frustration.

To earn a living during these war years, my father worked his camera in the parkland at the entry to the Redcliffe jetty, which jutted out into the shallow waters of Moreton Bay. This was where the huge hospital ships would wait off the coast, with thousands of war-weary and wounded servicemen onboard. Hundreds of these poor devils would be offloaded into smaller boats and brought in via the jetty. These were soldiers who had lost arms and legs and other parts of their anatomy. Many were blinded from shell blasts. Often horribly maimed, they were pushed in wheelbarrows and trolleys to the parkland. There, they regrouped to rest under the palm trees along the foreshore, while waiting to be transported to hospitals in the city and around the Queensland coast. The more mobile among them would have their photos taken by my father.

I was happy helping Dad at the jetty, though he would never let me out of his sight. Francis wouldn't help as she didn't like the sight of all those bloody bandages, so she spent these times playing with her mates.

The soldiers, particularly the Americans, often wanted a photo with me – the little Aussie girl all fancied up in a pretty dress – to send home. The African-American servicemen, who were often on a different ship to the white servicemen, seemed especially thrilled to have a little white girl in a photo with them. The little that I can remember of those times is my own thrill at having an African-American soldier hold me by the hand for a photo.

Over these few years in Redcliffe, Dad did very well as a photographer. At times he would take us to Brisbane to replenish his photo paper and equipment, and we would go to the carnival in Fortitude Valley and stay overnight. If my memory serves me correctly, the carnival was staged at Centenary Place Park, not far from the Story Bridge. We looked forward to these trips as the other show kids were there, and we would have great fun playing while Dad got together with his mates at the Valley Pub.

On one of these occasions, in August 1945, we had just arrived from Redcliffe by train and were walking down to the Valley when everything suddenly erupted around us. Horns were honking, tram bells were ringing and church bells tolling. People were hysterical; jumping, yelling and kissing each other. It was as if the whole world had gone mad. For all I knew, it was the end of the world. Then I heard the words people were screaming at each other: 'The war is over! The war is over!'

In the middle of this mayhem, I lost sight of my dad and my sister. I was engulfed by jostling, shouting people, all of whom seemed unaware of the plight of a small child. It was strange; after all my roaming alone, this time I felt overwhelmed. Then I remembered that the carnival was just up the road. I got over my panic and took off. Sure enough, there it was. It was such a comforting sight, all lit up and, to celebrate the good news, giving away free rides.

The carnival ran all night long. After six long years of terror and tragedy, World War II was over. The excitement was contagious. Oh, and Dad found me – and this time, I didn't even get a slap.

Chapter 9

A World of Our Own

1945–1951

With the end of the war, we were back on the road, using what fuel coupons Dad could get his hands on. A fair number of agricultural shows had started up again, and Dad felt it was time to make the most of them. Our first stop would be the show in our old stamping ground of Lismore.

Dad had acquired a rather fancy Pontiac sedan, manufactured in 1936, the year I was born. He was also lucky enough to have found a single-axle trailer that could easily be towed behind the car. The trailer was unusual in that it functioned as a basic caravan. It had a pop-up roof, with two single beds that pulled out on each side. The entry was from the back, leaving a good wide walkway, and cupboards built across the tow-bar end. My sister Francis and I shared one of the bunks, with Dad on the other.

My first glimpse of Lismore was of a big hill at the back of the showground. It was lush and green and, to me at least, gigantic! As a nine-year-old tomboy, all I wanted to do was climb it. But first I had to get through a barbed wire fence. I gathered up a team of show kids and away we went.

It was dark by the time the adults tracked us down atop that hill. I copped a belting for leading the kids astray. Francis – or Miss Goody-Two-Shoes, as I called my sister – had refused to climb the hill. I felt hard done by, but I knew deep down I was the most stubborn little bugger you would ever wish to meet. I suppose I was a little like my father that way.

The terrible news came through a day or so later. My sister and I were sitting with Dad at his photo stand when a local police officer walked up. 'Bert Bibby?'

'Yes, sir, that's me. What can I do you for?'

The copper handed Dad a telegram. 'The postmistress asked me to pass it on to you,' he said. 'Sorry, cobber,' he added, shaking his head and walking away.

Dad read the telegram. He ran his fingers through his hair and slumped his shoulders. 'Strewth. Not again.'

My sister and I just exchanged quizzical looks.

'Your mother is dead,' Dad said. 'Bloody hell. Well, that's that.'

Then he folded the paper, put it in his pocket and got on with his day. I felt a strange feeling in my stomach, like I wanted to be sick. But I ignored it and tried to do as Dad did, putting on a brave face. The show had to go on.

Our mother had died from a seizure. She had already been

interred in the cemetery at St Arnaud by the time the terrible news reached us. She was only thirty-seven and she'd been all alone. There was nothing Dad, or anyone, could have done.

Throughout that whole eerie day, I told myself I was lucky. Unlike my mother, I wasn't alone. I didn't just have Dad and Francis; I had all the show families. Later that night, I got lots of lovely hugs from people like Dolly Baker, who ran the burlesque show. I really liked the attention. While I was too young to fully comprehend the loss of my mother, I was happy to take any affection I could get! Dolly Baker even offered to adopt my sister and me, as she felt it was too much of a burden for my father to raise two little girls. Though the kind offer was declined, I was destined to grow up with people like Dolly looking out for me. As a motherless child, I would have many an 'aunty' or 'uncle' who would help educate me in some way.

I don't remember grieving for my mother. She'd been away for so long. Either I felt disconnected, or I was a showgirl at heart and knew that the only way to survive was to go forward. We didn't give in to sentimentalities. As for my father, he seemed even crankier after this. He drank harder and became even tougher on me.

After the Lismore Show, we headed into the Queensland outback to work the show run from Roma to Charleville, then up to Longreach and Winton. As usual, we travelled in a group of three to four show families.

Simply getting from one town to the next was a battle. While at the time we had to navigate without road markings – all signposts had been removed during the war to confuse the enemy should they invade – it was the roads themselves that proved the greatest challenge. They were rough as guts. This was black-soil country, where even a bit of moisture would turn a gully into a greasy, slippery quagmire. The only way to make it through the worst of these hazards was by helping each other out. Everyone, including the kids, had to push and shove to keep our convoy moving through the mud pits. We smaller ones gathered dry branches, leaves and grass from the creek banks for the men to pack under the wheels. Once we got a couple of trucks up on the dry road, we would then tow the rest of the trucks and vans out. We'd all be in good cheer, despite the mess and grunts and groans.

Our spirits were lifted all the more if some of the women went ahead in the first truck, so that by the time we made our destination for the day, there was a fire, a billy boiling and some of our favourite food: scones deep-fried in a pan of butcher's dripping. Dad called them 'floating bastards'. In New Zealand, they were known as Maori bread. When cooked, they would be lavishly spread with 'cocky's joy' (today's golden syrup). Yum. We needed the sustenance after that big haul, and to prepare for the next big show.

Arriving in a different town and campsite every week, we show kids had the biggest backyard in the world, with so much to see and do. We had a magnificent time of it, swimming and fishing in the creeks, climbing trees, and playing cowboys and Indians. If the weather was fine, we aimed to only come home to eat and sleep. On wet days we explored the sheds, pavilions and grandstands of each showground we stayed at. We were like little pack animals; where one went, all went.

But as we got older, we had to work, too. I prided myself on being able to do almost anything, from chopping wood to lighting a fire to carrying buckets of water to our camp. On show days, we were expected to work a game or sell tickets on a ride. From the time we were old enough to give change of a 10-shilling note, we worked show days. The rest of the week, we played with our mates and got up to mischief.

My best mates were Fred ('Bully') Walker, Johnny Miller and Doug Roberts. I don't think we ever stopped to consider that I was a girl among boys. I could do anything they could. I'd shoot and fish and swim with the best of them. You name it, I could handle it – including holding my own in a stoush. To warm up the crowd before the main event, I'd even lace on the gloves and stage a fight of one or two rounds with Arnold Bell – the young star of Roy Bell's boxing tent. My reward was a shower of coins from the happy customers, which often added up to a significant amount.

It was during these formative years, especially after my mother died, that I increasingly felt the brunt of my father's fiery temper. No matter how hard I tried to please him, I often ended up with a bruised or blackened eye. My sister fared better with our father, and I never really understood why. Perhaps it was because she was named after our brother Frank, who had died before we were born. Dad carried so much guilt from Frank's death. Or perhaps it was because Francis was most like our mother and I was most like Dad.

My father was often called a 'man's man', so maybe he thought he was toughening me up, to make me ready for life. While he could be harsh, I still had a vast amount of respect for him. I looked up to him even though I never got the kisses and cuddles I longed for. On reflection, I can see what a rough deal he'd had. He had lost two wives and three children. He had lost his buckjumping and circus show. He had to sell his beloved horses. And he didn't know where one brother was.

It was all I could do to keep trying to impress my father by being the son he no longer had. Through these years I learnt to load and unload Dad's truck, cook, clean, repair and build. I became proficient with all types of tools. It wasn't until I began to grow boobs that I realised I was a girl. When boys like Siddy Davis started trying to kiss me, I knew for sure.

Formal education was a strange affair for us show kids. Francis and I were sent to school at each town we were in. On arrival, we went to the headmaster's office to hand over our referral book, which showed the various schools we had been to, complete with our attendance record and achievements. We were then shown to a classroom and guided to our seats, which were mostly at the back. We had little hope of picking up whatever it was that the teacher was saying. Instead, we were usually given a colouring book to entertain us. That way, we didn't disturb the class. Nor did we learn anything.

At lunch and playtime, we endured the taunts of the town kids. They gave us hell, and many a schoolyard erupted into an all-out argument or fight. It was during this time that I decided that school was not for me. I could read and write my name; that was enough.

No more school. Oh, and those kids who gave us hell? We evened up on show day. They didn't win any prizes!

When I was twelve, in 1948, Francis and I began a whole new style of schooling. Dad decided it was time we girls were shown a world beyond sideshow alley. He spoke to Grace Sorlie, a very refined lady who was godmother to us both.

Aunty Grace was the owner of Sorlie's Revue, Australia's largest travelling vaudeville show. As we were travelling the same towns over the coming months, she said we could travel with the revue and learn to maintain the vast number of beautiful costumes that were worn on stage. At the same time, we could learn the art of dressmaking under the tutorship of the revue's wardrobe mistress, Gracie Le Brun – wife of Bobby Le Brun, then one of Australia's most famous comedians.

Sorlie's Revue was very upmarket. Before each evening's performance, Aunty Grace would arrive from her hotel in a chauffeured Bentley limousine to greet patrons. She wore an evening dress complete with diamonds and a fur cape. The public would be lined up, waiting to applaud her entrance. She wasn't called the 'Queen of Vaudeville' for nothing.

Over many months, my sister and I learnt how to use a sewing machine to make costumes for the vaudeville show. If I wasn't out tomboying with other show kids, I was up to my neck in sequins and beads.

The vaudeville tents hosted full-scale live travelling theatrical shows, bringing entertainment to the outback long before cinemas, radio or television arrived. In huge, canvas marquees, hundreds of patrons could be entertained each night by beautiful, scantily clad ballet dancers, acrobats, comedians and magicians. Dad made an extra quid taking photos of patrons with the girls. But heaven help any customer who tried to make a play for the girls.

By 1950, I felt I had learnt all I could from my vaudeville aunties. I was fourteen and ready to get on with my life. Like all good show kids, my goal was to own my own truck and equipment. To that end, I started my first show stall – a stock stand selling kewpie dolls on a stick, windmills and other toys classified as show souvenirs.

After working half the night sewing the dolls' dresses on a hand-driven, portable Singer sewing machine, and fitting the windmills onto sticks, I would work alongside my sister all the next day, selling these beautiful works of art to the show-going public. Francis hated sewing but loved working on show days, where she could flirt with the boys.

As for me, I wasn't really thinking about the opposite sex. I just dreamed of making my stand bigger and better. Besides, the things I saw some men get up to didn't exactly inspire me to want to hook up with them. If my father was anything to go by, I was better off without men in my life.

Arguing that he owned my stock stand, Dad started helping himself to the money my sister and I earned. He spent our hard-earned cash at the pub with his knockabout mates. In one way I felt he was entitled to a portion of our takings, since he was my dad. But it hurt like hell to watch him piss it all away.

The more this went on, the more I copped from my father after his nights of boozing with mates. If I dared speak up, he yelled abuse and slapped me around all the more. By this time, other show people often stepped in to stop the beatings as best they could.

After yet another set-to one night, I gave my father an ultimatum: if he didn't stop the heavy drinking and the beltings, I would leave.

The final straw came one evening close to Christmas, 1951. I'd had a great day at my stall and my money apron was full of cash. Dad walked up.

'Selling well?' he asked.

'Yeah, Dad, really well!' I said with a smile. Then, before I had a chance to blink, he snatched a wad of cash from my apron and took off. He was headed for the pub again.

That was it for me. I was sick of getting the rough end of the stick. It was time to look out for my own bloody self. I had not long turned fifteen. I wasn't a kid anymore. See yer later.

Off I went, shooting through like a Bondi tram, with the princely sum of £3 pounds and 10 shillings in my pocket. That was all my father had left me.

Chapter 10

Finding My Own Way

1951

Arriving in Brisbane on the Gold Coast train from Tweed Heads, I knew just where to go. I headed for Con's café, to the friendliest, kindest people you could ever meet.

Con and his wife – who we all called 'Mrs Con' – were originally from Greece and had come to Australia after World War II, opening a café in Stanley Street, Woolloongabba, on the south side of Brisbane. Con ran the front of house, while Mrs Con had complete control of the kitchen.

They settled me down with a great big cuddle and a good strong cuppa as I told them all my problems. Mr and Mrs Con knew the showfolk well, as they often catered for our various events (birthdays, christenings and so on). They also knew my dad and were well aware of his drinking problems.

Con was a mighty bloke; the kind of man you'd be lucky to

meet once in a lifetime. He and his wife made you feel like you could go to them whenever you needed help. I will be forever grateful to the Cons of this world.

After listening to my tale of woe, in between serving customers, Con arranged for accommodation for me at a nearby boarding house. For females only, it was at Kangaroo Point, near the Story Bridge and Brisbane River. Con also gave me a job as a waitress in his café. I'm pretty sure he also contacted my father, just to let him know that I was safe.

Con's generosity had me relieved and grateful, but I was scared all the same. I had never been so far from my family before. I had to remind myself that my father had lost the plot; that I'd had enough of the drunken verbal abuse, backhanders and thrashings I had endured since I was a little kid. I didn't know what the future held, but it was time to find a life of my own. I knew I had to grow up quick. I had to pass myself off as older than my fifteen years.

I started telling anyone who asked that I was eighteen, or I would shrug and tell them to mind their own business. It worked.

After a few weeks, Con asked about my plans. I told him I had no idea. I felt lonely and missed my friends. I hated the city. My life had always been in the country, at the various country shows.

Con hit on an idea. He arranged a job for me through the agricultural agents, Dalgety's Stock & Station Company. I would work with a family on a sheep station just out of Mitchell, a small town about 750 miles west of Brisbane.

After a long drive, I was greeted by the station owner, Pat

McCormick. He was friendly, but his wife left a great deal to be desired. She was an ex-model from Sydney and had tickets on herself. I had been hired as a nanny for their kids, who were both under five. But after a few weeks I found I was also hired as this woman's personal servant. She was the world's worst cook, so I was not only the nanny but the chief cook, bottle-washer and slave. The day she demanded that I get on my knees and scrub the never-used side veranda was the day I decided enough was enough.

I quit.

Pat McCormick was most understanding. He confided that they had never been able to keep house staff for any length of time. He also told me that the cook at the Mitchell Hotel had fallen ill, so the pub needed a temporary cook. That suited me fine, especially as accommodation came with the job. So, with Pat's recommendation, I became the cook at the town hotel.

You may wonder how a kid not yet sixteen managed this. Well, I'd been working since I was a motherless little kid and had mixed with much older people all my life. I had been cooking on a campfire since I was old enough to carry a bucket of water. My father had given me a set of butcher knives when I was twelve, and he had taught me how to use them. I learnt the art of keeping a fine edge on the knives. He had also taught me how to butcher a side of beef, lamb or pork, and to know every cut of meat. These skills were my key to earning a living. It was ironic that even though I could butcher, I was a vegetarian.

When I was due to finish at the Mitchell Hotel, the boss of

Dalgety's offered me a gig as a cook in the local shearing sheds. He admitted that Dalgety's were having trouble finding cooks, and they were prepared to pay top quid. He said the publican of the Mitchell Hotel had given me a big rap, although he was a bit worried about the shearers possibly creating havoc with me. Having been reared in sideshow alley, I didn't feel that would be a problem. I had a few tricks up my sleeve and knew how to handle all kinds.

A Dalgety's rep drove me to the first station a few days early to settle in. I learnt that there were seven separate shearing shed teams, all needing meals over the coming months. The weekly pay was £6, two shillings and sixpence – top wages – with all meals included.

I couldn't knock it back. Plus, if the men were happy with the food, I could expect a bonus from each shed from the men themselves.

I had no idea what I was letting myself in for.

For a start, I couldn't find a kitchen hand. This was a pity, as an offsider was needed for chopping the wood for the stoves, washing up, sweeping, cleaning, prepping vegies and so on. Not to worry. At the first shed there was only six men to feed, so not a problem. I could handle that, and I'd chopped wood before.

As for my accommodation at this first station, it was a lean-to beside the shearers' open-air shower, with a single bed and trough. There was no lock on the flimsy door. It was all standard for the times – most cooks were men or the wives of shearers. But even for a showie such as me, it was beyond the pale. After a long discussion with the station owner and the Dalgety's rep, it was agreed that I would stay at the main house.

The set-up was quite basic at all the stations where I worked: a big barn of an eating room, with the kitchen at one end complete with galvanised tubs for the washing up and tin buckets for water carried in from the outside water tanks. There were no fridges back in those days, and only just enough power from a generator to run lights. Outside was a wire mesh shed for hanging the meat away from flies. This shed, known as a cool room, was usually built under a tree for shade and to catch some breeze.

I got to work the following day. Luckily, the boss sent a man down to make sure I had enough wood chopped to start me off. There was plenty of meat to see the week out, so into the oven went a couple of legs of mutton, ready for the men's main meal the next day. Later, dampers and sweets were cooked. All men loved the sweets, especially bread and butter pudding or steamed pud and custard. All this was prepped up a day ahead. Thank God for what I had learnt during my short time in the Mitchell Hotel kitchen.

With the men due in that night, I made up a big batch of piping hot scones with a tin of plum jam and a huge pot of tea. I won them all over with this small gesture. They fell over themselves lending a hand. No problems with the wood pile or carrying buckets of water; they even squabbled over who was to help with the washing up. Also, none of them ever bothered me, if you know what I mean. This might have had something to do with the other thing I did that first night …

While they were scoffing down their scones and tea, I spoke up over the din.

'Shoosh up, fellas. You better listen up as I've got something to say. Glad you're enjoying those scones and my good brew. Now, just warning you. If any one of you tries on something funny with me, you'll all cop it. See those cups of tea you're holding and scones you're eating? Well, I'll put bloody epsom salts in those one day when you least expect it. You'll all cop it, you hear me?!'

Like I say, I never had any trouble. Some of these men followed on to other sheds I worked, where they let the new men know that any stepping out of line with me was not on, or I would spice up everyone's food with a good dose of laxatives. My reputation preceded me!

These same hard-working men, at the termination of each shed, would throw in anywhere from a couple of quid to a tenner each when the boss shearer took the hat around for an extra bonus for the cook.

The final shed I catered for was also the largest. Out of Bourke, over the border in New South Wales, it had sixty-four shearers for me to cook for.

For as long as I live, I will never forget the kind-heartedness of these men, nor the huge party they put on for me at the Bourke Pub at the end of the shearing run.

After all that, it was back to Brisbane for me, with a pocket full of hard-earned cash. At Con's Café, Mrs Con treated me like a long-lost daughter as I talked non-stop for several days. Once again,

Con came up with a suggestion. He had a cousin, Lenny, with a cafe where I could continue to develop as a cook.

The café was in New Farm, a suburb filled with single people living in boarding houses or flats, only a short tram ride to the city. All the cafés in this area did a very good breakfast and dinner trade. The kitchen of the café I was to work in was run by the owner's son Lenny.

Back in the early fifties, it was normal for breakfast to consist of two courses: porridge or Weet-Bix followed by bacon with two eggs and toast – cost was 5/6d (5 shillings and sixpence). Dinner would be three courses: homemade soup then the main course followed by a selection of sweets. This also included a pot of tea and all the bread and butter you could eat. There was no such a thing as frozen or fast food. Everything had to be cooked from scratch, right down to the apple pies that were a great favourite, served with homemade custard.

My workday started at 6am and finished at 8pm, five days a week, with a four-hour break in the middle of the day. Unfortunately, the break rarely happened as I usually had to pick up stock for the kitchen. None of this was a real problem until Lenny, a married man with children, started to put the hard word on me. He was constantly touching me in places he shouldn't have! With the wages basic at best, I certainly didn't need this harassment.

It was now early August and I had been away from home just on nine months. I was getting pretty lonely; I missed the companionship of show people. Life was hard out on the shearing sheds, but here in the city it was no fun at all. Determined to find a little joy between my shifts, I made my way to the Brisbane Showground where preparations were under way for the Ekka (Queensland's annual agricultural show, originally called the Brisbane Exhibition and then 'Ekka' for short). What a great day I had. Everywhere I turned, a familiar face greeted me, asking, 'What are you doing? When are you coming back? Do you want a job?' I realised that this was where I belonged. It was time to come home; not to my father and sister as such, but to the only life I really knew.

I was a half hour late getting back to work.

'Where the bloody hell have you been?' growled Lenny. He really dug the spurs in and let me have it. 'Who do you think you are, Queen Muck? You young sheilas reckon you can do what you want.'

We had an almighty blue in the kitchen. His poor old dad tried to intervene but to no avail. Lenny really went off his head. I left that day, heading straight for the place I knew I belonged – the Brisbane Showgrounds – and straight into a job!

Showman Ron Burns had a variety of games, but the one he wanted me to run was the Poker Roll Down. This was a pool game based on poker, and my job – apart from setting up and packing away each day – was to fill all twelve of the stall's long, narrow tables with players as quickly as possible to get onto the next game.

After agreeing to the handsome sum of £50 for the show, I went to work spruiking for all I was worth.

'Get over here, mate,' I'd call. 'Come on people, get over here.

Move your legs. Your body will follow! There's an opening right there. Put that lady in.'

I hustled and hurried potential customers like I'd been doing it all my life. 'Hey, look over here. Come on. Move it. You have to be in it to win it! There's a winner each and every time. It could be you!' Some people came on over just to check out this cheeky young girl.

With the show running for seven days and six nights, we would work from 9am through to midnight, plus a couple of days to set up then two days to pack up after the show.

On the fifth day of the show, disaster struck. I was flat-out spruiking on the Poker Roll Down game when a deafening explosion rocked the showgrounds. A short way down the show street I could see sheets of flames erupting from the games directly ahead. Next thing I knew I was running madly down the length of the show street, thinking *God help us, please God help us*.

With masses of people moving in all directions, a staff member had tipped the contents of a 4-gallon drum of petrol into a tractor's tank without turning the motor off. The tractor engine powered one of the larger rides. Something must have sparked and, with a blinding flash, the tractor had turned into a lethal bomb. Chaos followed. A row of gaming stalls was burnt to the ground, along with some of the children's rides. Some people were injured in the stampede that followed, while a worker was left with severe burns. Poor bloody mongrel. There was nothing we could do to help the man except get him to safety while we waited for the ambulances to arrive. All around was utter mayhem, with screaming and yelling from parents searching for their kids. I headed for the sideshow stalls, where some games were burning fiercely. Other showies were tearing away a sheet of burning canvas and hauling it into the open, where others had formed a bucket brigade. I jumped in with a group of show women and we soon managed to save a considerable amount of stock, piling it to one side. It was surprising how many of the show-going public also rushed in to help.

Drama and all, I was well worn out by the end of the show. I had worked a total of eleven straight days and nights, an average of fifteen hours a day with meals grabbed on the run. The only time my smile had slipped was when that explosion happened. Other than that, I kept up the brave and friendly face. As a showie, you never let on how tired you are; you just grin and bear it.

With the final packing finished, I went to collect my wages. Ron called me in and handed me a sealed bulky envelope. With a grin, he told me there was a 'little bonus' inside for all my hard work. He added that he would like me to run the pool game again the next year.

As I wandered away from the caravan feeling chuffed, I wondered just how much the bonus would be. I soon found out. When I opened the bulky envelope, there was no bonus – only forty ten-shilling notes, that is, £20. That was well under half of what we had agreed on. Strewth! That bloke was lower than a snake's belly!

My shouted tirade at Ron would have been heard from one end of the sideshow area to the other.

'You bloody rip-off! Can't trust you as far as I can throw you!'

Suffice to say, I got my £50. And I was pretty sure no one within earshot would ever mess with me again. I was learning very quickly that, showies or otherwise, not all people were honest or nice.

I needed to be with people who would give me a fair deal. Being on my own was not an option.

Having got a taste for spruiking, I felt this was where my future lay. I spoke to veteran showie Arthur Greenhalgh, who arranged for me to work the next two capital shows of Adelaide and Melbourne as a spruiker for a troupe of acrobats who had just arrived in Australia, direct from China.

Standing beside these amazing Chinese artists on the platform outside the marquee, dressed in black slacks and a red blouse, I spruiked with passion. Spruiking for a sideshow was different to spruiking for a game. With a game you had to be aggressive; this was more of a soft sell. I'd do a storyline that went something like this: 'Have a look at these astounding men and women who have come from one side of the world to another to entertain you, the show-going public. These artists will be performing balancing feats and acrobatic daredevilry that will take your breath away!'

I'd then focus on the main part of the act: 'This is a once-in-a-lifetime opportunity. You won't believe what you're going to see inside our huge marquee. Look at Charlie Chow there! Put your hands up, Charlie! An amazing contortionist, he is going to slide right through a ring of razor-sharp daggers, just like pictured there on the banner. Risking life and limb for your entertainment! One miscalculation and one of those knives could pierce his heart. There we have it, ladies and gentlemen. There's the pay box. In you go. The show is starting almost immediately. Hurry in now and get a front row seat. This is a show you cannot afford to miss. And one you will be talking about when you are many miles from here.'

It was all true about Charlie, too! The daggers were pointed toward the centre of the hoop, with barely enough space for his body to pass through. Just as well he was skinny as a rake.

Each show lasted a minimum of 20 minutes. Then it was outside again, with all of us back on the platform at the front of the tent, where the performers would give a short, eye-catching demonstration to the crowd that had gathered once again.

The Chinese troupe did very well at both capital shows. As much as I wanted to continue on with them, I had already agreed to work the Tasmanian show run, from October through to January, 1952.

The man behind the Tassie tour was Tom Castles. Recognised as one of the best sideshow spruikers in the country, he ran both illusion and burlesque line-up shows. For me, this was a golden opportunity to expand what little knowledge I had as a spruiker, and to travel throughout Tasmania.

Little did I realise what I had let myself in for.

Chapter 11

Off with Those Clothes!

1952–1953

I bounced into the dressing room full of vim and vigour, ready to show the waiting audience how good I was on a microphone. It was October 1952 and we had arrived in the north-coast Tasmanian town of Burnie. This was to be a full rehearsal. The show would start in a few days.

'Norma. Great to see ya,' said the boss, Tom Castles. 'Just head to the back of the stage with the girls and let's see how you go.'

To the back? How the hell could I spruik from there?

It dawned on me slowly at first. Then it hit me like a brick. I wasn't going to be a spruiker on Tom's illusion show. I was going to be a stripper!

'No bloody way!' I roared.

Tom started yelling at me. 'How the hell am I going to find a replacement now? The show's in two bloody days!'

After more yelling at each other, I dashed up to the stage curtain. I'll show them striptease! I'll give them an eyeful! Switching on the music, I ripped off my slacks and blouse. As a tantalising opening to my performance, I tossed my clothes through the centre opening in the curtain, where they landed in full view in the middle of the stage.

Then, showing only one bare leg and keeping in time to the music, I slowly rolled the curtain from my foot right up to my now almost bare thigh. I had pulled my knickers up as high as they would go. Twisting this way and that, I showed a bare shoulder and arm while the rest of my body was fully covered by the curtain. At the same time, I briefly let my terrified eyes check out who was watching. I then did a bit of a 'tease' dance, carefully draped in the curtain, without taking off any of my 'underneaths'.

When the music finally finished, I was in a lather of sweat. I then noticed that every showman from the Burnie Show was packed into the tent, and all were applauding wildly. The tease must have gone down okay! I did feel chuffed.

But this was definitely going to be my first and last public dance, and possibly even my job with Tom. I told Tom in no uncertain terms that I would accept a pay cut, but no way was I going to become a stripper. My dad, if he found out that Tom had hired me to strip, would kill us both. And Tom knew it! I don't know what he'd been thinking.

Tom managed to fly in a professional stripper from Melbourne to perform in the tent for the duration of the run. Whew.

And that is how I almost became a stripper for the first and only time. After my temper tantrum I realised that this was my life. I had been born into the world of show business. It was a vital part of me. And whatever the future held, it was up to me to make it work. I had to put this situation right.

I did this by becoming the best spruiker Tom Castles ever had. When I wasn't spruiking, I was selling tickets or making or mending costumes. In other words, I was more than pulling my weight. By the time we returned to the mainland in late January 1953, Tom and his wife Shirley had become my close friends. And they completely supported me as I took up my next adventure – spruiking for a famous fan dancer.

Paula Perry and her husband Mick operated a daring sideshow called Paulette the Fan Dancer, with Paula the sole performer. I had known Mick Perry all my life. He was from the old and well-known Perry's Circus. The couple had heard about my striptease fun and games in Tassie (as had the rest of the show people) and suggested I come and spruik for them on the New South Wales show run into Queensland. Paula reckoned that if I could handle Tom, I could certainly handle the yobbos who sometimes skylarked around her tent.

My accommodation was to be in a screened-off portion of the lean-to attached to the Perry's caravan. Paula offered to further my education by teaching me to read and write properly. Bonus!

Working with Paula and Mick, I learnt proper microphone technique and developed the ability to enunciate my carefully chosen words. I coaxed customers to the ticket box, rather than just yelling at them over a loudspeaker. Paula did the rest, aided by ostrich feathers. Constantly teasing her audience, she allowed an alluring view of her moving 'nude' body. Bending, turning and swaying in time to music, Paula's fan dance came to a climax as she stepped behind an almost sheer curtain and removed both fans, giving the now madly applauding audience a tantalising glimpse of her fully naked self; she was in fact wearing a sheer body stocking. The whole performance was titillating and bewitching from beginning to the end.

A fascinating character who had danced her way across the world, Paula had been in Manila on a world tour when Japanese forces invaded the Philippines, attacking Pearl Harbor the same day, in December 1941. Paula's troupe was trapped. The Japanese herded thousands of people, including Paula and her fellow performers, at gunpoint into the University of Santo Tomas in the Philippine capital. Interned, they spent the war years locked in the university auditorium until their release in 1945.

During this time, the prisoners formed a theatre and school group to keep the internees, especially the children, entertained and educated. At first, all believed their internment would only last a few months. As the months became years, they clung to the hope that the Allies were winning the war, which they eventually did.

On her release, Paula returned to Australia, where she joined the Tivoli Theatre run by George Wallace Snr. This was where she polished up her fan dance act, along with her Ostrich Bird Contortionist performance. With Mick Perry as her husband and manager, Paula began wowing audiences all over Australia with her Paulette Show. Its motto: 'to conceal and never to reveal'. This was the true art of the strip and tease dance, and nobody understood it like Paula.

Chapter 12

Comedy and Tragedy

1953–1954

With our run of Queensland shows finished in August 1953, it was time to say goodbye to Paula and Mick. They were going to take a long-deserved rest at their home in Sydney. I planned to have a break away from the major shows by following the country show runs, where I could work on various games. There was no shortage of work. I knew I'd always land on my feet.

Though I sometimes made do in cheap boarding houses, more often than not I stayed on the showgrounds with friends and their families. It was a great life.

It was the end of December, after I'd had a few weeks off in the Entrance, north of Sydney, when I was approached by Jack Gill of Gill Bros Rodeo. The Gills were showing the various towns along the northern coast. Jack asked me if I could help him out by taking care of his wife Gladys, who was terribly ill with cancer, and maybe do a little cooking for the family. How could I say no? I had known the Gill family all my life.

Before the Gill Bros show started, a group of us teenage showies decided to head into Kings Cross for some fun. Off we went, eight or ten of us, aged seventeen or eighteen. We hit the high spots, prominent among them the you-beaut girlie shows. I saw sights I had never seen before. There were bare boobs jiggling and bouncing all over the place, and bare bums. The covered bit on the front didn't hide much. Yahoo! The boys loved it.

It was after midnight by the time we headed back to Moore Park, where a carnival was set up just outside the Sydney showgrounds. I was staying there with my good friends Ivy and Snooky Godfrey, while I worked the Sydney show once again with the Chinese Troupe.

I must admit that we were all making a bit of a racket, what with hands travelling everywhere and kissing and cuddling. We were having a great time until Ivy Godfrey played 'Mother Hen'. She put her head out of her caravan window and yelled, 'What the bloody hell's going on? Don't you kids know the show starts tomorrow?!'

Our shenanigans came to an abrupt halt, and I lost my first almost-boyfriend. And almost my virginity.

My first few weeks with the Gills went well, though cooking for 'the family' was a big ask as it included not only Jack and Gladys, but also their three sons and an entire crew of roughriders. Everyone got well fed and I even learnt to sit on a horse, with a great deal of help from Margaret, the lady buckjump rider. I felt like a real cowgirl.

By the end of the month, I was incorporated into the show as the assistant to the sharpshooter. Then, when Margaret broke her arm in a bad fall, I was informed I was to be the new lady rider. Bloody hell. I had only just mastered the art of sitting on a horse! After my pleading not to do it, Jack Gill assured me that I would only be on the horse for a few seconds before being pulled off by one of the outriders.

Idiot me. I started out as a cook, then I was being shot at in the sharpshooting act, and now they wanted me to bust my guts on a buckjumper? Even with the outriders' helping hands, I had Buckley's chance of staying on a bucking bronco! Well, it was on regardless …

The ringmaster Jack Gill announced my debut into the microphone: 'Now you've seen our Brahman bull in action. You've seen the exhibition rides on the Ghost and the Wild Mouse and our roughriders on champion horses. You've got to admit it's been an action-packed show. We'll now conclude with our lady rider, Norma Bibby, riding our wild, unbroken buckjumping brumby, Joyful.'

With much applause from the audience, a rough-and-ready brown brumby was led kicking, snorting and snapping into the stall. The bit was quickly slipped into its mouth and the saddle was clinched on. The boys did their best to quieten this beast from hell. The audience gazed on in awe as I climbed to the top of the crush and dropped into the saddle. Utterly terrified, I prayed to my God that I might get out of this alive. Then the attendants swiftly jumped from the crush and swung the gate open. I shut my eyes, only to open them again in wonder: Joyful was no longer a snapping, snarling brute. He was leaning against the wall of the crush with his head drooping, half asleep!

I'd been had. And it seemed the horse was in on it too! The audience burst into laughter. The team had all had their fun, and I went along with the gag. Upon dismounting, I gave Jack a deep curtsy and the attendants a stiff-fingered wave. There really is no business like show business.

The following year, during the Sydney show of 1954, my nerves would be put to the test yet again. At seventeen years of age, I was asked by Arthur Greenhalgh of Greenhalgh & Jackson's to train as a motorbike stunt rider, on the Great Wall of Death. I had seen this incredible act when I was about fourteen years old. I vividly recalled the announcer with microphone in hand and the smell of petrol fumes tickling my nostrils. The Wall of Death show was performed by The Barcolas, a husband and wife motor stunt rider duo. It was an exciting, multi-sensory experience. But it was also terrifying. In 1952, Mrs Barcola (real name Una Langmead) died after a crash on the Wall of Death at a carnival in St Kilda, Melbourne. This was the same type of Wall of Death that Arthur was now asking me to train for.

No doubt reading the expression on my face, Arthur said, 'Don't worry, Norma. What happened to Mrs Barcola will never happen to you.'

And that was supposed to be reassuring! What was I to do? Well, what we showies always did. It was drummed into us as soon as we could walk: the show goes on. Besides, no one was going to call me chicken!

So began my new life as a travelling stuntwoman. I was assigned to a caravan with a great mob of girls as we headed west over the Great Dividing Range and into Bathurst, in preparation for the first show on the New South Wales country run. Along the way, my roommates kindly gave me fair warning about men's wandering hands during shows – even when those hands were meant to be busy controlling motorbikes. Since I was going to be riding pillion at first, I didn't think it would be a problem.

Over the next few months, it was non-stop training. The motorcycle champ Bobby Crompton was to be my partner in the act. Joined by the chief rigger, Jack Howth, Bobby took me inside the Great Wall of Death to begin my tutoring. The 'wall' measured 24 feet high and nearly as wide, built as a straight up-and-down perpendicular timber cylinder. Near the top was a 3-foot wide platform, complete with safety rails. A staircase was fitted to this platform. About seventy or eighty patrons would gather around the top of this vast, circular wall to watch the show from above.

'See that ramp, Norma?' said Jack. I saw an angled timber ramp attached inside the wall at the base. 'That's going to support the motorbike as Bobby races around on it until the bike builds up power to jump from the ramp onto the wall. Bobby and you will be leaning sideways away from the wall as he performs his stunts.'

I looked up at the wall. It was horribly high.

'See that wire?' he continued. 'That's your safety line. It will stop the motorbike from flying over the top. We don't want to fly into the crowd, do we?' I spied the cable, angled inwards, about two feet from the top of the wall. Hmmm. That was the same type of safety wire that Mrs Barcola's bike had clipped before she and the bike had parted ways and it fell on her.

'Don't worry, Norma,' said Bobby, as he placed an arm around my waist and gave a little squeeze. 'You're safe with me.' Hmmmm. I was starting to wonder about that.

For the act, we didn't wear helmets. I simply wore black trousers, a white shirt and a 6-inch-wide belt. The belt supported my inner organs and also made the whole outfit stand out. Though there was no safety gear to speak of, I didn't feel nervous. I told myself that the lady rider's death had been a freak accident. I knew that letting any fear or doubt into my mind would jeopardise the act.

The hardest part of working inside the cylinder was the noise from the revving motorbikes in such a confined space. It was deafening and near impossible to hear directions. We communicated with hand signals, which made the learning process longer. Bobby had some hand signals that I certainly was not comfortable with. Just as my friends had warned, his hands roamed everywhere, and he was always making innuendos about what he'd like to get up to with me. And it wasn't about riding a motorbike!

After working our way along the New South Wales South Coast, our final show before the Christmas break was to be in Queanbeyan, near Canberra. For the last performance of the day, showing to a packed house, Bobby's hands were busier than ever as he helped me onto the bike. I warned him that I would tip him off the bike if he kept it up. 'Back off!' I said, finally. It was time to put a stop to his shenanigans. And I knew just how to do it.

The final act on each performance was the Dive of Death, performed with us both on one bike. But this time would be different. We were racing at high speed around and around the very top of the wall, barely missing the safety wire. As we dipped down into the Dive of Death, I slid my hands under Bobby's armpits and started tickling. The bike started swerving all over the place at high speed, up and down the wall, in not one but a whole series of dives. Bobby was struggling to regain control, but I was laughing my head off. No-fear-Norma!

Thinking this was all part of the act, the audience were screaming in amazement at this sudden, spectacular finale by these two crazy daredevils.

Finally, coming to a standstill at ground level, Bobby and I managed to take our shaking bows.

'You're bloody crazy, woman!' Bobby shouted. I responded with a death stare.

I was later told that this was the best stunt ever performed on the wall.

From then on, I performed solo.

Chapter 13

My First Truck

1954–1955

'I'm getting married!' Francis was squealing down the end of the phone. It was towards the end of 1954, and my sister's long-time boyfriend, Arthur 'Happy' Wood (the son of old-time vaudeville showman Bill Wood), had finally popped the question.

'You're going to be my bridesmaid,' she said. 'And you have to wear a dress, you hear me? A pretty one. And get your hair done.'

With the wedding set for March 1955, around the start of the New South Wales show run, I assured Francis I'd be there and do as I was told. I was happy for my sister, but I couldn't really relate – I had no interest in getting married.

Bossy Francis then threw in her punchline: 'Oh, and Norma? You're going to have to stay and take care of Dad now. He's nearly seventy, and you know his health isn't the best. He can't travel alone anymore.'

Dad had given up photography and was now working a small hoop-la game. He got around in a Ford ute, towing a ten-foot caravan that my future brother-in-law had built for him.

With Francis having spoken, it looked like I had little choice. After a couple of years as a solo stunt rider, it seemed that my free-wheeling life might be on the skids. But like my difficult father, I wasn't so easily tied to one place.

At Francis's wedding I had my first and only experience of wearing a bridesmaid's dress. Held in a Catholic church close to Newcastle showgrounds, the wedding was a huge event, with Happy's extensive family and show people from all over attending. What a celebration. And the food! Mountains of it, mostly cooked up by the show women in their caravans. And I must say, I did look pretty!

After the wedding I worked the annual Newcastle agricultural show, where my family saw me ride on the Wall of Death for the first time. My father's reaction was: 'Harrumph, not much different to riding a buckjumper.' I heard that down at the pub that night, though, he never stopped giving me a rap.

Without raking over our difficult times together, Dad and I seemed to be friends again. We headed south to work the Bega-Cooma show run, with Dad continuing to work his hoop-la game and retaining his independence.

Then, on the last day of the Bombala show, I was struck by gut pains so bad I could barely handle the bike on the wall. It was appendicitis – less than two weeks before the Sydney Royal Easter show. Didn't I say earlier that there's nothing easy in show business?

I was operated on in Bombala's tiny country hospital. With no keyhole surgery back in those years, I woke with plenty of pain, and stitches.

While I was recuperating in hospital, Dad moved all my gear into his van. As soon as I was released, we took off in the Ford ute and caravan, arriving in Sydney just in time for the opening of the show.

My first port of call was to Arthur Greenhaulgh's office. Although I had contacted him by phone from the hospital, I wanted to apologise in person for being unable to work the show. After warm embraces from everyone in the office, Arthur told me to rest up and not to worry.

'But be ready for the Ekka in August,' he added. 'Your replacement will be finished by then.'

As the weeks passed, Dad and I settled our differences. We had to, as we were living in close confines. He had the bed and I slept on the dining table, which lowered into a single bed each night.

But even on friendly terms, we couldn't do it for long. I needed more room and privacy. I figured I needed a truck. A bedroom could be built into the body for me, and there would still be plenty of loading space for equipment.

With what I could have earned at the Sydney show, I would have had enough capital. But now, with no income, what could I do?

I turned to my godfather, Dave Meekin, for help. If anyone could solve my problems, it was good old Uncle Dave.

A good boxer in his day, Dave quit the ring in 1921, having won, so he claimed, a fair number of titles as a welterweight. He went on to become a boxing tent showman, but he failed to survive against the much stronger troupes who monopolised the more lucrative shows. Dave then conducted a variety of 'in and out' sideshows, such as Goliath the Monstrous Bull and Wee Jimmy, the smallest racehorse in the world. During this time, it came to Dave's attention that a showman, Tom Fox, was having a big problem with the pygmy woman in his show. Her name was Ubangi Chilliwingi. She was from Cape Province in South Africa, and she couldn't, or wouldn't, speak English. As it turned out, Dave had learnt a smattering of the woman's language, Afrikaans, having travelled in Africa during his fighting career.

Dave and Ubangi hit it off, and a successful show partnership began, with Ubangi billed as 'The Smallest Woman in the World'. She became part of Dave's family – calling him 'Daddy' or 'Baba', while he called her 'Bubby'.

Over the years, Dave brought out many other little people from Africa, all of whom would give exhibitions of spear throwing and tribal dances. As all members of the troupe were on temporary work permits in Australia, Dave travelled back and forth with them to renew their visas every year.

Dave was a very keen showman and his would be the first show to open and the last to close. Walking up and down in front of his beautifully illustrated jungle banners, he would constantly call for patrons to enter the tent. 'Come one, come all. This may be the only chance you'll ever have to see these fascinating little people, direct from the jungles of deepest, darkest Africa.'

(By the late 1960s, the freak shows had lost favour, and Dave retired to live in Kings Cross. Ubangi became an Australian citizen, living on the Gold Coast with Dave's daughter Beryl until her death.)

Arriving at Uncle Dave's sideshow tent, I went straight in to see dear little Ubangi Chilliwingi – or Maria, as we showies knew her. I adored Maria. As a little girl, I used to help her clean her caravan. She was too tiny to reach the top cupboards, but never too tiny to give me a huge cuddle. If the other show kids gave her any trouble, she would scare the bejesus out of them by chasing them with a tiny spear. She never let on that she could understand every word they spoke. She was always one step ahead of them.

When I found Uncle Dave in his office, I laid my cards on the table. I told him I needed space from my father and wanted to buy a truck.

After some deep thought, pacing the floor with his head down and his hands in his pockets, Dave finally came to a stop in front of me. 'Well, young lady, does your father know you're here?'

'No, Uncle Dave,' I answered. 'He wouldn't have allowed me to ask you.' We both knew Dad would have been too proud to let me go begging for help.

After a bit of muttering under his breath, Dave once again came to a stop in front of me.

'You've been a bit crook lately, haven't you?'

Before I could answer, David said, 'Well, how much do you

need?' I caught the gleam of mischief in his eye. I answered, '£200 will be enough, Uncle Dave.'

He was already peeling banknotes off a large roll from his pocket. 'Two hundred quid won't be enough. You'll need travel money.' He added another fifty quid.

As I was trying to thank him, he said, 'Pay me back when you can. And don't tell your father.'

Well, that was a given!

The following Sunday, I took off to Newtown with my brother-in-law Happy, who'd found a truck he thought would fit the bill.

The owner was asking £550, but we got him down to £475. Not a bad price for a three-tonne 1938 tray-top Bedford, which was in pretty good condition as it had been stored on blocks (hidden from the army) in a shed throughout the war years.

I was as happy as a pig in mud to have my very own truck, though learning to drive it was no easy task. With the old unsynchronised 'crash box' truck gears, you had to match the speed of the truck to the speed of the engine every time you wanted to shift gears. Dad, who assumed I'd bought the truck with my savings, battled to master this art with me. We just kept clashing gears, and tempers. In desperation, and after many choice words, I told Dad I would find a driver, at least until we smoothed things out.

This time, I went over to the showgrounds in search of Dick Riley, a handy fellow from an old show family. I was pretty sure I'd find him at The Hole in the Wall, a bar run exclusively for show people.

Another old-time showman, Jim Delaney, had opened 'The Hole' on the Sydney showgrounds during the Royal Easter Show after the end of World War II. He'd found an old storage shed at the back end of the Hordern Pavilion, well out of sight of the general public. The front door was hanging off the frame and the place was full of rubbish, but the space appeared to be waterproof, and the show society agreed to let Jim use the shed on an indefinite lease. When one of Jim's mates suggested that the storeroom would make an ideal drinking spot, 'The Hole' was christened.

The showmen would gather there, hidden away from the bustle of the show area, with bottles of ice-cold beer. Before long, there'd be a game of dice or two-up, a song or two, and of course a few tall stories. With Jim's wife, Liz, cooking up meals for the show people out of her gazebo-style food stall, it was a great place to unwind – especially after a day that started early and didn't finish until around 11pm for the ten days of the show. Liz's gazebo was situated just so – the front of the stall serving soft-drinks, fairy floss and donuts to the general public, while the other side dished out meals for the showies as they enjoyed a quiet beer, or several.

While the tradition began at the Sydney show, The Hole eventually took its place on the Queensland show runs, mostly in the railway yards during the long nights of loading the show equipment. In later years, as rail travel started to drop off, The Hole made its move to the showgrounds. There, it was set up in the rear of Harry Riley's Suction Gun Game and was known as The Guzzling Hole.

One of the longest-running operators of The Hole on the Queensland run was Stanley Green, who ran the place with an honesty box, which is still used to this day. Known as Stanley's Box, it has a message on the side which reads 'Way in to stay in'. The meaning being 'no change given' – whatever money goes in, stays in.

(After Stanley passed away, Johnny Davenport took over, eventually followed by Rodney Phillips, who ran a diner/hole/card night, then Shane Blades, with help from a few of the boys. My daughter Kym ran it for a couple of years in the 1980s, but had to give it away as it was hard staying up most of the night and then working all day with her diner. From there, the boys took over once again – this time, Luke Chambers, Boyd Baker and Josh Evans, with a few others. More than seventy-five years after the first Hole was opened, it's still going strong. Rossi's Hole, on the north run, and Tommy Baker's Hole, on the lower run, live on – with all profits going to the various showmen's clubs.)

Back in 1955, I don't think anyone imagined The Hole would outlive so many of us.

Sure enough, Dicky was at The Hole that day when I went looking for him. I pulled him aside and asked him straight out, 'What plans do you have for after the show?'

After a little umming and ahing, Dicky finally replied, 'Oh, I suppose I'll head north or something. Whadya have in mind?'

'Well, Dick, I've just bought a truck. Not much of a load on it. If you like, you can throw your gear on and drive it for me. I reckon I can feed you as well.' Since Dad liked a tipple as much as Dick did,

I added, 'And I know Dad would like your company.'

Dick's hand shot out and the deal was done.

We were ready to roll, more or less. The truck provided all the room I needed for my motorbike gear, but it wasn't ideal for living in. As it was a tray-top, it had no cover to keep the weather out. Until I could afford a proper covered-in body, my living quarters would comprise a ridge pole with a canvas tarpaulin over it, laced down firmly. Dick even set up a small roomette for his quarters. With everything loaded up, we were all set to go, with Dad following behind with his ute and caravan.

As I was still recovering from my operation, I wouldn't be working on the Wall until the next Brisbane show in August. So, the decision was made to double the size of Dad's little hoop-la-game, with both of us working it for the North Queensland show run.

From Sydney, we drove to the small township of Stroud, which had a little one-day show. Then it was on to the Kempsey show. We did well at both shows and were looking forward to the next stop, the three-day Grafton Show, when trouble struck. As we drove onto the Grafton showgrounds, the truck's engine started knocking. Dick immediately cut the motor off.

All I can say is thank God for good mates. Our fellow showies came to the rescue, led by 'Snooky' Godfrey. This showground scallywag had grown up to be a self-taught mechanic and all-round handyman. His first question was, 'Did you drain and replace the oil?' Our negative answer was all he needed. Snooky turned to Dad. 'I think you've done a piston. I'll know better when I've pulled the head off. Let's drag it over to that empty shed. The weather looks a bit dicey.'

I was more than upset. Here was my beautiful truck with a blown-up engine. One of the men helping put his arm around my shoulder. 'It'll be okay, love,' he said. 'We'll get it going again.' His words, and his lovely blue eyes, were reassuring.

By that evening, Snooky had dismantled the engine and found the trouble. Wandering over to our camp as he wiped the grease from his hands, Snooky spoke in his usual laid-back manner. 'You threw a ring off the piston. It didn't score the block, but only because Dick had enough brains to cut the motor. Next time, change the bloody oil.'

Snooky and his helpers worked through the night to repair the truck. These were the type of men I knew well: on one hand working half the night and refusing any reimbursement, while on the other giving you a dressing down for being an idiot.

Back on the road not long after, I decided it was time I got a driver's licence. Dick was still our chief truck driver, but that wasn't about to stop me. With our camp set up, Dick drove me to the police station. I won't say the name of the town. You'll find out why soon enough.

While Dick took himself off to the local for a pint, I waltzed into the station to smile sweetly at the sergeant behind the desk.

'I'm after a driver's licence,' I said.

'Are you, now?' he replied. 'Where are you from?'

'I'm with the show, camped down at the showgrounds.'

'Ah, more show people,' he said. 'Can you drive?'

'Course I can. I'm a good driver!' I thumbed at the truck parked across the road.

'You can drive that?'

'Sure can.'

'Well, I suppose I better take you for a run,' he said. He was about to get up when he noticed me slowly sliding a £10 note across the desk.

And with that, thank you very much, I walked out of the station with my licence.

'See you at the show, Sergeant,' I said as I went.

I went straight down to the corner pub and ducked my head inside. (In those days, women couldn't go inside or they'd be arrested.) 'Let's go, Dicky!'

'Okay, Norma. I'll just finish this beer.'

On the way back to the showgrounds, Dick asked to see my licence. 'That looks fair dinkum!' he said. 'You can't even change the shift on this old clapper. How did you do that?'

I grinned with pride. 'I did it with a £10 note!'

Chapter 14

My Handsome Hero

1955

After the Grafton show, which was a bit quiet owing to wet weather, we decided to back-pedal to Coffs Harbour, north of Sydney, for another three-day show.

While at Coffs, we gathered up all the showie kids for a day out at nearby Moonee Beach. With the younger children in the shallow, sand-banked pool, we much older 'kids' took off for the deeper water.

All the while, there was this one fellow who kept trying to get my attention. He was a fair bit older than me but, golly, he was handsome. Blue eyes and brown hair, with a smattering of grey coming through. Nice and tall. And … woo wee … he was really well-built! He kept on playing around underwater and teasing me. Of course, I pretended not to notice him.

Sometime later, after having a good long swim in the deeper

water, I looked around to find I was all alone. Where was everyone? Bobbing up and down with the waves, I finally caught a glimpse of all my friends, way back on the beach. They were waving frantically, but I just thought they were being friendly. I waved back and started showing off, diving up and down with the waves. The next thing I knew I'd been grabbed. A huge pair of arms flipped me onto my back and started dragging me back to the shore.

I didn't take kindly to being manhandled. I vowed to punch the living daylights out of this bloke! Getting to my feet in the shallow water, my arms were like windmills. I was swinging left, right and centre, while hearing him laughing. What the hell was going on? My mates were all laughing too … possibly in relief. Somebody reckoned they'd seen sharks out in the deep water, and this chap had swum out to save me.

It was only when I'd caught my breath that I realised exactly who this brave chap was. It hit me like a rogue wave. Not only was he the man with the lovely blue eyes who had helped repair my truck, he was the man I'd seen fighting nearly to the death about five years earlier, outside the Maryborough pub! Mick Brophy had disappeared from the showgrounds soon after that fight, but I hadn't forgotten him, or the wildness in those blue eyes. Only now, I saw something different. Now, he was my hero, and he was going to be mine.

I never did tell Mick that they weren't sharks swimming out in the deep with me; they were dolphins.

Mick and I had our first date that very night, at the cinema in the little town of Maclean, up the road from Moonee Beach. I think the film was about a horse and rider crossing a desert, though I wasn't paying much attention. We finished up sitting on the theatre steps, talking about what we wanted out of life, and about each other.

Up until then, my big plan had been to have my own business within show business. Where I was going from there, I had no idea. I just wanted to get more gear to load onto the truck, I suppose. I had never thought about a boyfriend.

Over the following weeks, we were hardly apart. I learnt that my man's official name was Alfred Roy Brophy but, being of Irish decent, he'd long ago been dubbed Mick.

Of course, there was more to learn than that. We both knew this was no time for keeping secrets.

I got to asking him about that fight. 'You nearly bloody murdered each other,' I told him. 'And then you just disappeared.'

Slowly but surely, Mick filled me in on his life. This man who was to become my husband had been to hell and back.

Mick's life early 1940s–mid-1950s

Mick was reared in the Perth suburb of Subiaco. His dad was head bartender at the Savoy Hotel in Hay Street for more than twenty years, until his untimely death in Mick's teens. Mick's mum had passed away some time earlier. With two older brothers serving in the armed forces, and a sister working 12-hour shifts in the local munitions factory, Mick was left to fend for himself.

Faced with few options, he did what a vast number of other young men had done before him – he lied about his age to join the army. At only sixteen, he and several mates were speedily shunted off to Darwin. With minimal training, they were deemed ready to be shipped to the Philippines, where the battle against Japan had begun in earnest.

When it was time to board the ship, all the young men were lined up and the sergeant in charge started the call, running his finger down the list. Suddenly he stopped and bellowed, 'Mick Brophy! Step out of line!' Now how unlucky can you be? The sergeant in charge just happened to be Mick's older brother, George.

Mick wasn't allowed to go to war, but since Darwin was a war zone, he couldn't leave. So he was stuck in the barracks and not allowed off base. He couldn't even get paid because, being underage, he was no longer officially enlisted. Mick became a courier on the base, delivering mail and doing whatever jobs could be found for him. He had no choice but to wait it out until he turned eighteen, when he would be automatically conscripted back into the army.

He was still underage when, on 7 December 1941, Pearl Harbor was bombed by the Japanese and nearly a month later, the Philippines was also taken. The problems seemed to be insurmountable. In Darwin, it was complete chaos. But the day Mick's war started was the day the Japanese attempted their invasion of Darwin, on 19 February 1942. On that day all hell opened its doors and Mick was right in the middle of it. After the massive clean-up and only months after his eighteenth birthday, a traumatised Mick was shipped to the Philippines, and even deeper into the Japanese war zone.

From the moment he landed in the Philippines, Mick and his fellow soldiers were gambling with their lives. It was a dog-eat-dog existence. Mick found that even when he was pulled back from the frontline, his life was in the balance. There was no such thing as a safe haven, and no man could dodge the bullet that had his name on it. When the day came, Mick was found in the bottom of a foxhole with major wounds to his back and legs, the bullets having missed his spine by millimetres.

It was some months before a ship was available to transfer all the war-wounded back home to Australia, where Mick underwent more treatment in Adelaide.

Within a few weeks of coming home to Perth, Mick collapsed. He was found to be suffering from 'shell shock' (now classified as post-traumatic stress disorder, or PTSD). He was admitted to the Claremont Mental Hospital. There, he had electroconvulsive therapy to treat the severe depression that had overwhelmed him.

Released from hospital, Mick found himself wandering around Fremantle, where a fun parlour caught his eye. He struck up a conversation with the showman owner, Fred Miller (better known as Fred Milo), who was having a bit of trouble moving one of the heavy slot machines. Mick offered his help. By the end of the day, Mick had become a member of Fred's staff.

On Victory in Europe Day, 8 May 1945, less than a year out of hospital, Mick married Fred's daughter, Goldie Alice Milo-Miller, in the Basilica of St Patrick's in Fremantle. (Legend has it that more than twenty-five couples were married in the cathedral that day.)

When Fred offered his son-in-law some gear he had stored from the old carnival days, Mick put together some games and riding devices – after some hard work and a lot of spit and polish. This enabled Mick to work at carnivals in and around Perth. Having learnt the ways of show business, and with Fred frail with heart problems, Mick soon took over the running of the outfit. Poor old Fred died soon after.

It was around this time that Mick invented a new show game.

For many months he had been searching for a factory to make wooden balls for a knock-em-down game. In the traditional knock-em-down game, three or four wooden balls would be thrown at a pyramid of wooden blocks. If you knocked all the blocks down, you got a prize. It was a game for the men. But factories were still closed following the war. So what to do?

One day, while strolling through the main pavilion at the Perth show, Mick noticed a stand displaying different types of wool from Western Australia's various breeds of sheep. Samples of each wool type were stuffed into little cotton covers. These wool-filled balls gave Mick a bright idea. He knew the balls were too soft to knock over a stack of hard wooden blocks, but they could work well at knocking over something lighter.

Mick 'borrowed' a couple of these balls and, after a night spent testing his theory, he was ready to give the world a game he named The Tin Can Alley. The game was set up using three empty baked beans cans on the bottom, with two shorter cans on top, forming a pyramid. To win a prize, punters simply had to knock the pyramid over, using two soft, wool-filled balls.

The new game was an instant success, especially because it could be played by mums and kids, not just the big tough men. I can confidently say that my husband invented the first ever soft ball and tin can knock-em-down game.

Even so, it was still a pretty tough life as a showie following the war. With the population of Western Australia not even hitting the half million mark, the small country towns were struggling. Carnivals were few and far between.

By 1951, with a growing family – two little boys, Michael and Fred – Mick and Goldie decided they should head east while they still had enough capital. Goldie's mother, Amy, would join them. They would tackle the long drive in a couple of ex-army trucks, helped along by motor mechanic Tommy Poland (also a returned solder and a long-time friend of Mick's).

To drive the Nullarbor Plains is to take on one of the longest, flattest, straightest roads in the world. The Eyre Highway seems to go on forever. But back then, it was a road of gravel, dirt and deep corrugation. It was smothered in bull dust that seemed to penetrate every stitch of clothing. With no hint of air-conditioning, the heat on such a gruelling drive was immense. For Mick and his group, with two little kids and constant mechanical problems, it was sheer agony.

After more than two weeks, and about 2500 miles (4000 km), they made it to Coffs Harbour. But the journey had taken its toll on

Mick and Goldie's relationship. The couple had been at loggerheads on the road and were all but ready to call it a day.

Mick settled his family into a large carnival where Sandy Moore's Boxing Tent was the main drawcard. He then headed down to Sydney for several weeks' work with Bill Bowler, an old friend from Western Australia, at the Royal Show. Bill had a surprise waiting for Mick. Among the games he was running for the show was Mick's own, The Tin Can Alley. It was now going to be seen for the first time in the eastern states, with Mick working it on a two-out percentage deal (meaning a fifty/fifty split).

Flush with success from the show, Mick went back to Coffs to try to repair the marriage. But when he got there he found that Goldie had taken up with Sandy Moore. Six years down the drain; he was only twenty-seven. What the hell was he going to do now?

Mick figured he may as well head north for the show run in Queensland, though the break-up had started playing hell with his nerves. He had left so much behind – his wife, his boys and his dreams. He had left all the carnival gear with Goldie, who would need it to earn a living and feed the kids.

Over the next few months, Mick roamed around the show circuit, working various stalls for whoever would have him. He also took to the booze, having fallen in with a team of other young guzzling show people. These travelling, carousing blokes formed a drinking club called The Nyngan Boys (inspired by a particularly rip-roaring night in the central New South Wales town of Nyngan). For men only.

From there, Mick was on a roll. Working by day, pub crawling by night. Nothing could stop him. By the time he and his hard-drinking showmen buddies arrived in Maryborough, Mick was up for anything. Even taking on a hulking, enraged drunk from Sharman's boxing troupe. Just for the hell of it.

A few weeks after that unforgettable fight, the inevitable happened. Mick had a complete breakdown, finishing up in the Goodna Mental hospital in Brisbane.

For four long years, Mick remained there. Those were his lost years. It was no wonder I hadn't recognised him when I saw him again. His hair had turned from jet black to silver grey. But to my eyes, he was still the most handsome man I had ever seen. I guess in a way you could say he found himself when he found me.

Being a tomboy, I only wore a dress on special occasions, like when my sister Francis (left) and I got dolled up for a fancy portrait shot at Bert's Hollywood Studios in 1941.

We certainly had our differences as sisters, but we both loved a trip to the beach. This is me (left, aged 13) and Francis at Burleigh Heads, during the Christmas carnival of 1949.

Like all good show kids, I longed to run my own show stall. Here I am (left) in 1950 with my very first stand, selling kewpie dolls, with my sister Francis. The trick was stopping our father Bert (centre) from skimming our profits! Not long after this photo, I took off to make it on my own.

This is my father, Bert Bibby, circa 1952, with a show baby he was taking care of for the day.

As a young show woman in the early 1950s, I found I had quite a knack for spruiking. Here I am in 1953, mic in hand, pulling a crowd for Paulette the Amazing Ostrich Fan Dancer.

It's not me in this picture, but this is a similar Great Wall of Death to the one I used to earn a crust on as a motorcycle stuntwoman.

Here I am, aged 17, about to tackle the Great Wall of Death at the Queanbeyan Show in 1953. Beside me is my co-rider Bobby Crompton, keeping his hands to himself for once.

When our show trucks got bogged, everyone pitched in. It was an all-too-common problem on back roads such as this one near Gundagai, circa 1953.

Show trains like this ran from Brisbane to Cairns from the 1930s to the 1960s. The excitement was contagious as we showies pulled into each town, with our circus on rails all ready to be set up.

In the early 1960s, Mick dreamed up a 'Lucky Envelope' game with towering walls of prizes. We were on a winner.

Me, spruiking the striptease: 'These girls will make your shirt race up and down your back like a venetian blind.'

Me and Mick celebrating our long-awaited wedding in 1971. We had one hell of a party!

Though no easy feat, it was only natural that these kids would grow up learning the art of circus performing. A proud Mick and me with our sons Gary (15), Warren (13) and Ashley (12).

At just 15, our youngest, Ashley, was already a fearless tightwire wonder. Here he is at Redcliffe Showgrounds in the early 1980s, accompanied by Warren, juggling on his unicycle.

Me doing what I do best: still spruiking, after all these years!

Our boy Ashley practising his skipping on a highwire at our property near Bendigo, in preparation for the Flying Angels act. One miscue and he could be split in half.

Norma's GALLERY

Being a can-do showie, I was handy with a brush from a young age. Here's me doing some touch-ups to my Slim Dusty portrait, painted on an old tent canvas.

Whether it's with a microphone, paintbrush or pen, I've always been interested in sharing my stories. I was motivated to start painting scenes of my show heritage to capture these memories for posterity. I was thrilled to be contacted by the Canberra National Library of Australia, which has transferred my catalogue to their Pandora Archive, where it will remain in perpetuity. I hope they jog happy memories for everyone who sees them. Visit: www.carnivalart.com.au

Who's Up for the Challenge?

In this painting, Roy Bell is spruiking for contenders to muscle up and box their way to number one. The supervisor is Roy's son Arnold, who I used to spar with as a kid to draw in the crowds.

Ashton's Circus

It's all hands on deck when erecting the famed giant Ashton's Circus tent. When my daughter Kym saw this painting, she said, 'I'll take the bundle of muscle on the far right.'

Taking a Peek

A few cheeky onlookers enjoy a free show. A typical sight in the 1950s.

The Showies Campfire

Everyone loved the camaraderie around the glowing embers as music played and tall stories were told. Those were the days! The truck in the background is my first truck, complete with living quarters.

Yesterday's Sideshow Alley

This painting is of the first agricultural show held in Melbourne after the war years, in September 1946.

Wet Day at the Show

Amid one of Australia's worst droughts in 2007, the heavens opened for show time. It rained for the duration of this show at Mackay in North Queensland. But rain, hail or shine, people always rolled up!

Chapter 15

Cycle of Life

1955–mid-1960s

'Who does this Mick Brophy think he is?' My father was shouting and swearing, waking everyone within earshot.

It was around dawn, and I'd just wandered in after spending the night with Mick. I told Dad that Mick was a good man; that he and I had something special.

'He's an imbo,' Dad replied, using the cruel old slang for 'imbecile'. 'He's just out of the nut house. He's not the full quid!'

My father had an answer for everything. But his ranting wasn't going to get to me. Not after the night I'd just had.

Mick and I had had a wonderful time, talking and cuddling and getting to know each other (in more ways than one!), all while sitting on a narrow bench seat in the tiny cabin of my truck, with a gearstick jabbing at us. It was our last night together before Mick had to hit the road, to drop off gear in Brisbane for his outfit with Billy Bowler.

Despite the obvious attraction, Mick told me he was worried about the difference in our ages. He was almost thirty-two and I was not quite nineteen. I could well understand his concern, as in his lifetime he had touched the gates of hell. He kept pointing out that in time he would be an old man, while I would still be a young woman.

After Mick had left, I'd headed back to my camp, happy but sad, straight into a hornet's nest. Dad had been waiting for me. And that's when I copped it, and the name calling started. I think he used every adjective that had ever been invented.

It was Mick's ex-wife Goldie who barged into our tent to shut Dad up. 'Righto, Bert! That's enough. Give the kid a break!'

A large woman with a determined manner, Goldie then grabbed me by the arm and shuffled me from the tent. 'Go and have a cuppa or something, Bert,' she said. 'Norma's coming to my van, and she's not coming back until you calm down.'

Over the next few weeks, Mick and I managed to keep in touch by public pay phone, as he was still on the western run. We talked again about the difference in our ages, the fact that he was still a married man and how he felt that he had nothing to offer me. He was completely honest. He also pointed out that my father was well and truly against us seeing each other, mainly because of Mick's breakdown.

In the meantime, Goldie and I became unlikely friends (we were the talk of the showgrounds). After more than five years without Mick, she was happily settled with her boxing tent showman, Sandy

Moore – so much so that they had had two little girls together, Sandra and Maria. Goldie said she and Mick had never been well-suited; that theirs was an overexcited wartime wedding. They shouldn't have married in the first place.

Goldie's blessing meant one less hurdle for me. Things were looking up. But still, my life was like a galloping merry-go-round – one minute up then the next minute down.

Over the next few months, during the coastal show run, Mick and I were together constantly. His troubled past didn't mean a thing to me, even though a few show people insisted on warning me that a man like Mick could erupt at any time. I was even told that any children I had with him could be born mentally deficient!

Of course, I also had to contend with my father, who was still trying to turn me off Mick. At least Dad quickly learnt that it was no good him talking age differences or marriage status, as my answer was that Dad himself had been twenty-five years older than my mother, and that they had never been married. For much the same reason, he could hardly criticise Mick for being a booze artist. Fact was, Mick was now a social drinker only, unlike old Bert. And besides, Mick was a hard worker, without a lazy bone in his body. All up, I figured Dad was only against this new man in my life because it meant I might not be around for him. He'd have to fend for himself.

It was during this time that Mick and Bill Bowler, who were still partners, moved onto the same run as Dad and I. For my part, I not only loved Mick, I also trusted him completely. I felt I'd always be safe with him. I wanted him to be the father of my children and I knew in my heart that he would be a great dad. Plus, he was a grouse looking sort. Ask anyone.

We soon got engaged, at the Rockhampton show. Mick bought me a beautiful diamond ring and officially asked Dad for my hand in marriage. Dad could see the writing on the wall. He knew that nothing he could say or do would change my mind.

Our next step was to have Mick and Goldie's marriage annulled. But we found that to hire a barrister and go through the court system would cost a hell of a lot of money, with no guarantee of success. Money we didn't have. Divorces were often only granted for exceptional reasons back in those days. The divorce plan had to be shelved; for how long, we had no idea. But we were determined to eventually walk down the aisle together. We just didn't know how long our engagement was going to be.

When Dad smashed his ute and van beyond repair around this time, it was no surprise to anyone. He'd always been an erratic driver. But it now meant I had to share my little 10-foot-square tent with him. Adding to our woes, Dicky Riley quit, leaving me with no driver. After a brief lesson from Mick, and with his assurance that he would always travel right behind me, I took on the role of truckie. After all, I did have a licence!

In Mackay, Mick found an old Pantech shell which, with the help of a few mates, was fitted onto the tray of my truck. I then turned my hand to carpentry. (If my father taught me anything, it was that no handyman job was impossible. I'm sure he thought I was a boy through those early years!) With little more than a hand drill, saw and hammer, I put together a tiny walled-off room – the very first bedroom I had ever owned. With a lockup door fitted, I had complete privacy. Pretty soon I had it decked out with a second-hand wardrobe, drawers and even a full-sized mirror! There was lino on the floor, and I painted everything a soft cream colour. After several late nights at the sewing machine, I had a patchwork quilt of many colours for the bed, with lacy window curtains completing the arrangement. Mick and I did have some fun in there, unbeknown to my father.

Finishing the north show run at Cairns, we made the long drive to Brisbane, with Mick tailing me all the way. We both worked the Ekka in early August, with me fulfilling my commitment to Greenhalgh & Jackson by performing on the bikes.

After watching me perform as a stuntwoman, Mick put his foot down heavily: 'This is the last time you will ever ride the Wall of Death!' He was terrified that I would crash and kill myself. He also couldn't understand why my father had allowed me to risk my life this way. So that was the end of my stunt riding.

Following the Ekka, Mick and I both had a pocketful of money. We decided that since Mick had two games and a fair bit of stock, we would load it all onto my truck and he could live in the tent with Dad until the divorce came through. He made arrangements with Bill to end their business partnership and go solo. I wasn't game enough to tell Dad our plans for Mick to travel and live with us. The first he knew of it was when we headed for Sydney and Mick climbed into the truck cabin with us. For the whole cosy drive, Dad only answered when spoken to, and sometimes not even then. He well and truly had the shits.

In Sydney we got Mick's gear out of storage and loaded it quickly, before heading directly to our first show together at Parkes, on the way down to the Victorian run. We had been on the road all the way from Brisbane for a very silent four-and-a-half days. The old man was barely talking to us, even though we were now formally engaged to marry.

I know we were both in the wrong by not telling him that Mick was going to travel with us, but we were not openly living together 'in sin'. I didn't know how to alleviate the problem and convince Dad that if we were to get enough capital together to buy a caravan and earn the money for Mick's divorce, this was the only way.

By the tail end of October, we were in Albury, on the New South Wales–Victoria border. Dad had finally seemed to accept that sharing the tent with Mick was working out, and that Mick and I were going to make a go of it one way or another. He wasn't going to be kicked out.

Just before the Albury show, Mick heard about a caravan for sale. It was 15 feet long, had leadlight windows and was fitted out with twin beds, an icebox and a two-burner shellite fuel stove. It was a delight and, at £800, a steal.

With Mick picking up the caravan on the last day of the show, I figured it was time to move all of Dad's gear into my little truck room. Mick could then have the tent to himself. Well, guess what? When I stepped into the caravan, Dad was lying back on one of the beds with a smart-arsed grin on his face. He had commandeered my beautiful new caravan. He'd already moved in bag and baggage. This was payback!

Okay, I thought, *So he wants to play that game.* Dad and I had lived together in his original 10-foot caravan for years. At least this one was larger and fitted with two single beds. We would just have to share. And at least now I wouldn't have to drop the table each night to make my bed. Plus Mick could have the truck room, and we could do away with the tent. Take that, Dad. Let's see who wins this bout!

After the run in Victoria, we had a bit of a break before starting up our own Christmas carnival. Showman Tom Whittingslow suggested we hold the carnival at a bayside beach outside Melbourne named Black Rock. Since we didn't own any kiddies' rides, Tom offered us a couple of his own to use. For food, we contacted Paddy and Mary Hector, who would bring their canteen. Mary was originally of the McDonald fairy floss family and Paddy was a former boxer who fought under the name Paddy Slavin. He was a good mate of Mick's.

We thought we had a great carnival, though we ended up earning only just enough money to survive. Business was so slow at times that it felt like the locals who fronted up only did so because they felt sorry for us!

It was while we were running the carnival that I realised I was pregnant. I had been feeling off colour for some time. This was a pretty mess; there was nothing else to do. Dad had to be told.

Strangely enough, he was quite okay about it. It was a sign to me that he had finally accepted Mick.

That night, while we were packing up, Dad moved all his clothes out of the caravan. Without a word, he stacked his gear into my old bedroom in the truck. We took that to mean that Mick could move in. It was 2 January 1956, and from then on, Mick and I always regarded it as the day we officially became man and wife.

Of course, back in the 50s, you didn't dare move in with a man without being married; it was just not done. What were we to do? Well, our mates saved the day. If anyone asked, either Mary or Paddy would immediately concoct the story of our beautiful wedding, with the Hectors as matron of honour and best man. This warmed our hearts: no money but great friends, and a baby on the way. What more did we need?

We had great plans for our little unborn bundle. If it was a girl, we were going to name her after both our mothers, with Mick's last name: Violet Venetia Brophy.

But in early March, while working the Bega Show south of Sydney, I was overcome by stomach pain. Though I tried to ignore it and push on, I soon collapsed. I was rushed to hospital and straight into surgery. I had a ruptured fallopian tube from an ectopic pregnancy. Sadly, we lost our baby.

For the first time, I discovered what true heartbreak really felt like. Mick took it very badly, too. He had really wanted a baby. He'd missed the early years of his two sons, who were aged two and four when the marriage broke up and he was later admitted to the mental hospital. Goldie and the boys now were often on different show runs, so Mick rarely saw them.

For both of us, losing our baby was a painful blow. Why did life have to be such bloody hell? Fortunately, the stars were soon shining down on us once more: I was pregnant again.

With Mick off at the Sydney shows, I was camped at Rosedale Caravan Park, Sydney, doing my best to take it easy. This was going fine until one morning when I went to get something from the back of the truck, only to find a strange man hidden under one of the canvases. I got the shock of my life. I grabbed a stick and started yelling. 'Come on, mate! Out you get!'

Hauling this fella out, I had a good look at him in the light. He was in his thirties, in ragged clothes, with no shoes on. He was filthy, and by god he stank. The smell of him! He mustn't have bathed in months. Or if he had, it was in a bathtub of liquor.

'Now you get over to that camp there, where the blokes are sitting, and stay there,' I ordered.

He knew to do as he was told and stumbled off. Meanwhile, I got him a change of Mick's clothes and some shaving things.

I told the fella to go have a shower and shave, change into fresh clothes and then come back to me for a feed and chinwag. He followed dutifully, perhaps due to the promise of a meal, or he was just that scared of me. As he gulped down his meal and a hot cup of cha, I learnt his story.

His name was Milton, a returned airman. After he'd demobbed, he'd headed home to find his wife had moved another man in.

Milton didn't take it well. He went on a bender, laying into the drink like it was water.

Originally from Tasmania, Milton was an accountant by trade. But now he was destitute. I couldn't leave him like that, even though at a glance he seemed like a real warb – that is, a useless individual who doesn't want to work.

'Listen, Milton,' I told him, 'you've got a long life ahead of you. So, get up off your arse and get on the straight and narrow. You need a job? Well, you've got one now. You're working for me.'

From then on, Milton did our bookwork. He was one of the best workers we ever had. He was brilliant with the numbers. I just had to throw a list of figures at him, and by the time I got the last number out, he'd have already totalled it up.

Milton became a close friend to both Mick and me. So close, in fact, that we asked him to be the godfather to our two little girls. Yes. Two girls. In June 1958, we were blessed with a beautiful little girl we named Anita Shayne Brophy. She was lovely in every way, with the right number of toes and fingers, a gorgeous complexion and snow-white hair. Our heartbreak was eased – all the more so with the arrival of beautiful Michelle Kym, who we called Kym, in July 1960.

Now, while it might be assumed that we showies are not overly religious, we are into our traditions. And we do like our kids to be christened. Christenings, birthdays and even funerals are a chance to bring us all together. So, Mick and I decided to get the girls christened. Simple, right? Having chosen Milton as godfather and our friend Betty as godmother, I headed down to the local Catholic church in Carlton, Melbourne, to knock on the presbytery door. The resident priest, as Irish as could be, invited me in. God help me if I could understand his accent! He was so excited to know that not only was I from the showies at the carnival, but that I also wanted *two* babies christened. Two for one!

I gave him the girls' names and ages. All good. Then he wanted my details.

'Of course, you are Catholic, aren't you?' he said.

'Yes, I am.'

'So, where and when did you get married?' I said we were married at the Melbourne registry office.

'The date?'

'I can't remember, Father.' I was starting to get worried about these lies.

'Never mind, we'll soon find out. So, you are Catholic. And your husband?'

'No, Father, he's not. He's Presbyterian.'

That's when everything hit the fan. 'He's not Catholic?!' The priest then said that in the eyes of God, we were not properly married. (If only he knew that we weren't married in anyone's eyes but our own.)

'You'll have to get married,' he quickly said. He had it all worked out. 'We'll rechristen Mick and we'll marry the two of you the following week.'

By this time, I was tearing my hair out. How could I get out of this? I was in big trouble.

'Oh yes, all right, Father. We can arrange that.'

'Good,' he said. 'Now, the godmother. She's Catholic?'

'She's Church of England.'

The priest took a deep breath. 'And the godfather?'

'Oh, he's Jewish, Father.'

Up in the air his arms went. 'This will never do! We will have to provide you with some of our nuns as the godparents. We cannot get past this.'

'So, we can't have our chosen godparents?'

'Certainly not!'

That's when I made my exit. I made an excuse that I had another appointment, and I ran out the door.

Back at the carnival grounds, I told Mick and Milton everything that had happened. We had to laugh. We could only imagine what the priest would have said if I'd told him that Milton reckoned his full name was: Milton John James Charles Aloysius Henry Victor Mervyn Moore.

We did end up getting the girls christened, in the local Presbyterian church. They were happy to welcome us, and all the showies who turned up!

Later, when we told Mick's sister about the christening story, she couldn't stop laughing.

'What's so funny?' I asked.

'Norma, Mick's not a Presbyterian. He's a Methodist!'

In 1962, our first little boy came along: Gary. Like the girls, we registered him under Mick's surname even though we were still not married and there appeared little hope of this happening as there was no money to spare.

We had just finished a show in Lilydale, on the outskirts of Melbourne, when Dad took ill. It seemed the hot weather had got to him. He was admitted to St Vincent's Hospital, with the doctor assuring us that the old bloke just needed bed rest.

We set off to work the Lorne Beach carnival for the Christmas season, knowing Dad was in good hands.

A week later, we got the call. Dad had passed away in the early hours from deep vein thrombosis. It was November 1962. Dad was seventy-eight. We were shocked. There'd been no warning. We thought it was just heatstroke. Knowing the old bugger as we did, we could only assume he'd been suffering from other issues but hadn't said anything.

We quickly organised a funeral befitting this old showie. My sister Francis flew down from Brisbane and we laid Dad to rest in Melbourne's Springvale Cemetery. Many show and circus people attended. RIP Albert Emery Bibby.

My father had been a horse breaker, sharpshooter, roughrider, bare-knuckle fighter, spieler and photographer. As a showman, he had worked countless games in sideshow alley. He had lived through two world wars and the Great Depression, travelling far and wide by horse and wagon, then by newfangled motorised vehicles. In the process, he lost two wives and three children, and as an aging father went on to face the greatest challenge of all, rearing two very young, motherless daughters.

Sure, he was rough on me occasionally, especially when going through his most challenging times. But really, I don't dwell on that. (In fact, I'd almost forgotten until I dug deep to write this memoir.) He did the best he could in an era when emotions around life's disappointments were constantly swept under the carpet. Sometimes, those emotions blasted out in a moment of anger or a swig of beer, but life went on. And so it did now for me and Mick and our three kiddies.

Chapter 16

Bigger and Better

1960s

Over the next few years, we expanded our show business, adding extra games along with another truck and car. We also bought a big 22-foot caravan from Hughie Miller, a showman who made plaster ornaments as prizes for our shows. It was a great caravan, with a lounge that could convert into a bed for the little ones and a kitchen complete with an electric refrigerator. It also had a separate bedroom and an undercarriage guaranteed to tackle any road.

Our new living quarters inspired me to come up with one of the first ever shower-baths in a caravan. This was done by removing a few of the cupboards and replacing them with a galvanised tin base, sealed up by a plumber, complete with an outlet plug. It had 12-inch-high metal walls to form a bath. After we waterproofed this compartment with lino, I hung a curtain in the doorway to stop the water splashing out. Job done. Well, almost. Mick then came up with a brilliantly simple way to supply hot water to the shower-bath. A big tank was fitted onto the van roof, with a shower head and tap protruding through the ceiling. We heated the tank water using an electric immersion heater, although the sun often did enough to give us a quick shower.

It was around this time that Mick woke me, as he often did, to tell me about a new idea for a show game. There was never a dull moment with that man! He was forever the quiet designer, who was always dreaming up new ideas.

He excitedly explained his plan for a game of chance that cleverly overcame the problem of cramped space in your average show stall. 'If we can't go lengthways, why not go up?' he said.

The next day we started building. We made twelve timber boxes which, when bolted together, formed a huge 12- by 24-foot display wall. The boxes were stabilised with props in the back. Once the wall was erected, we fitted a canvas veranda roof, making the height even more imposing. By filling the boxes with a variety of prizes, we used this background for Mick's new 'Lucky Envelope' game, in which a player was invited to pick a winning ticket.

It wasn't until many years later that this game was updated and built even higher, to become known as 'The Jolly Giant', owned and run by the showie Charlie Gardner. The Jolly Giant was stocked with all types of new prizes, such as giant teddies and other stuffed toys. This style of show game remains extremely popular to this day.

Our new game was ready for the Benalla Show, in north-eastern Victoria, where it attracted players from early morning until late in the night. Within a few weeks every showman raised their stalls from the normal height of 6 feet 6 inches to 8 feet high. The biggest fear was wind and rain, but as Mick often said, we worked in fine rather than inclement weather most of the time. This was a gamble we could take.

In this era, every child would win a prize on one of these eye-catching games. With crowds at record numbers, it was a time of bigger shows and bigger prizes. The food stalls expanded to keep up with demand. They were now in caravans known as canteens, with shutters from one end to the other.

Making the most of the good times, Mick also tested a golf game. The idea was to putt golf balls down a long, felt platform set up like a golfing green. The more balls you putted into the hole at the end of the table, the better the prizes. This proved to be a great game for the daylight hours but not good during the more important night hours. After a good trial, we gave that idea away. However, some years later, a showie named Frank Foster operated this game at the 1978 Melbourne Show, where he claimed to be the original inventor. He lost money on it.

Mick's ideas kept coming. We now had several games – hoopla, knock-em, two shooting galleries, pick-a-box and a floating duck game. Having taught myself to wield a paintbrush over the years, I now seemed to be forever signwriting new banners for these games or cooking for the men on our staff, although I never had to wash up after the meals. The staff were great, and the water drums were always full. They were also great babysitters.

(As it turned out, Mick wasn't the only inventor in our family. Some forty-five years later, our daughter Kym, just for a laugh, set up a stall she called 'Power Ball'. The name was a take-off of a TV games show. The idea was to set up the Tin Can Alley game, but instead of using the usual two small softballs, you had to knock the complete stack down using only one huge 10-inch plush toy ball that was much larger than the stack of cans to be knocked over. This game worked remarkably well for some time, but like many other games before it, it eventually faded away.)

With the 1960s a boomtime for showies, it was hard to keep up the supply of prizes for the stalls in sideshow alley. Luckily, we had some wholesalers who provided exclusively for showmen. But even then, stocks sometimes ran short. We were always looking for more and better prizes for the players to win. Our ornament maker Hughie Miller worked day and night manufacturing plaster prizes.

For toys, china figurines, kewpie dolls and other top-shelf prizes, suppliers Pat and Joe Feillia were the people to see. A fellow by the name of Ian Fleming was the man to go to for a great range of boxed chocolates, including sweet treats labelled 'Nudie Cuties'. (Chocolate was such a staple at the shows that the Cadbury chocolate factory even put out a special edition 'Old Gold' chocolate box dedicated to a showman, Jack West, who ran the 'Kicking Donkey' game.) From the Raddin steel factory in Sydney came beautiful stainless-steel horses. If you were lucky, you could win a full set, and you could only win them at the show.

It was also during the 1960s that a new breed of prize became popular, due to a bit of a misunderstanding. It happened at the Townsville show, where husband-and-wife showies Val and Bluey Seymore worked their roll-down game. To win a prize, a player had to roll a billiard ball to knock over two packs of cigarettes. When one particular bloke did just that, he started looking around the stall to select his prize. He pointed to a cage with a budgerigar inside. With Val in tears, Bluey finally convinced the gentleman that the budgie wasn't up for grabs – it was Val's pet. And that's how a new type of prize, a live budgie, came to be at the show.

Through these busy years, we travelled some of the roughest roads in Australia with our kids, staff and expanding show set-up. On leaving Victoria after our annual Christmas carnival season, we would head up through western New South Wales and on into the Queensland outback. After the western show run, we would head back to Brisbane for the Ekka in August, followed by the Adelaide show in South Australia and across the mighty Nullarbor Plains to work the Perth show. Finally, we'd arrive back in Victoria for their country show run. Then we would start our journey all over again.

In this way we were often part of the migration of sideshow, rodeo, circus and vaudeville people. On occasion, the sideshows featured top-line country singers such as Tim McNamara, Buddy Williams, Ron Peters, Tex Morton and Slim Dusty, many of whom later ran their own shows in the town halls of the outback.

On the north Queensland run, singers such as Normie Rowe, the Bee Gees, Johnny Farnham, Chad Morgan and the LeGarde twins performed in sideshows owned and operated by the old-time showman Johnny Foster, and his son Frank. From the mid-50s and throughout the 60s, most of these fantastic singers became household names thanks to the exposure they received as performers in the tents of sideshow alley.

In the many months in the outback, and after work on show days, these singers would look forward to our campfires, where they would plan hunting trips in the bushland with Mick and other showmen. On these trips they brought back ducks, geese and the mighty wild boars – enough wildlife to feed all the show families. Later, as we travelled further into the more open plains, the men would return after a great day of hunting with huge plains turkeys. One of these was big enough to feed two families.

But food was the last thing on anyone's mind the day we were flagged down by Tim McNamara, one of Australia's country music pioneers. We were driving across the Nullarbor from Perth – Mick in the Bedford and me in the station wagon with our kids and staff split between us – when we saw Tim frantically waving his arms and yelling by the side of the road. 'Stop, Stop!'

Tim had just finished performing at the Perth show and was travelling with three of his crew in his big Pontiac. Like us, he was heading back east for the Victorian country run of shows.

It turned out that Tim had stopped for a young husband and wife who desperately needed help. The young woman was in labour. The baby had come early, and they were in a right pickle.

Back in those days, you were lucky to see another vehicle travelling this road on the same day, so to say this young lady was happy to see a group of women was an understatement. My Mick soon had an awning rigged where I quickly had the girls on our staff make up a bed for the young lady. A fire was set up, with boiled water at the ready for the birth.

While cuppas were handed round, and Tim played uncle to our kids, I guided the young mother through labour. I'll spare you the messy details. Let's just say that some hours later, after a fairly easy birth, her husband had the pleasure of cutting the cord and having the first cuddle of their newborn daughter. The next morning, Tim got the trio through to the Cocklebiddy roadhouse, where they were well looked after until the Flying Doctor arrived.

Tim told me later he was sure I'd know what to do as I'd given birth three times. Smartypants! He seemed to remember me mostly for my birthing talents!

On another trip, a different kind of emergency tested my nerves. We had headed to the Northern Territory for a carnival that a few showies had put together at an Aboriginal mission out of Mataranka, famous for its thermal pool, in Elsey National Park. We had taken only the one truck and caravan, and the road was little more than a bush track with many creeks and gullies to cross. One of the biggest crossings was Roper River. It seemed shallow enough but, to be on the safe side, Mick said I was to drive as he walked the crossing with a long stick poking and prodding, looking for any soft spots or deep washaways. I was about halfway across when Mick leaped right out of the water, churning across the creek and screaming at the top of his voice, 'Croc! Croc! Croc!'

I'm not sure, but I believe I beat him to the other side. There wasn't just one croc. I will swear on a stack of bibles that the one I saw had his mother and his father with him as well. We arrived at the mission in record time, to the great amusement of the Aboriginal people who hunted these waters.

Chapter 17

Wild Acts and Adventures

1960s

We were ready to head west for the Perth show one year when Mick heard of a sideshow that was for sale. We had plenty of sideshow space to erect a large tent and, as Mick pointed out, I was a darn good spruiker. Better still, we could have it ready for the upcoming Perth show.

The overheads for running games were getting steep for us by now, as each stall had to have someone to work it, and every stall had the same type of prizes on them. The days of the plaster statues were fading. With this new sideshow, we could cut our overheads almost in half. We even managed to do away with one truck permanently, so travel expenses were also cut. But as far as I was concerned, the biggest attraction of this new sideshow was the fact that on show days, I could have my fourteen-month-old baby Gary in the ticket box with me. Anita (who we called Shayne, using her middle name) was now four and Kym two.

The tent show that Mick bought was known as 'Wanda the Underwater Girl'. After paying a small admission fee, the public would enter the tent to see a tiny, miniaturised girl, only six inches high, living, breathing, eating and sleeping underwater in a goldfish bowl. Was she real or a figment of your imagination?

Not surprisingly, the Wanda Show proved a real money spinner at the Perth show. We even had to hire a bouncer to control the huge queues that formed to gaze in wonder at Wanda. This was a great little sideshow, which hugely entertained people of all ages. Funny that years later there was a Monty Python movie named *A Fish Called Wanda*!

On the long drive back after the Perth show, another idea for a show slid into view. As usual, I was driving our station wagon far ahead of Mick to allow some of the billowing Nullarbor road dust to settle. Travelling with me were Sandie Shaw and Colleen Roach, who worked the Wanda show, and the three little kids. We weren't long out of Cocklebiddy roadhouse when I spotted a large brown snake lying in the middle of the road. I hopped out of the car and grabbed the snake, moving it well off the road.

Mick pulled up in time to see me farewelling the snake. 'What the bloody hell do you think you're doing, Norma? Is it poisonous?'

I pointed out that in my time with Greenhalgh & Jackson, I had spruiked on the snake show and often helped put the serpents in their travelling crates at pack-up time. I told Mick that the snake was only sunning itself and was not doing any harm, although it could have been run over. With no more thought about it, I continued on my way.

A couple of months later, Mick came up with the brilliant idea of opening a snake show, with me as the reptile handler! Whatever happened to the man who was so fearful of me killing myself in a motorbike act?

First off, I painted a new set of banners. And, as I felt that Norma was a pretty mundane name, I decided to call myself 'Natasha the Snake Girl'. My next job was to machine sew a heavy-duty canvas pit, where the reptiles would reside on show days. About the size of a small swimming pool, it was 5 feet deep and surrounded by a high platform for the public to stand on as they gazed down at me in awe.

On show days I dressed in my old motorbike gear, a very comfortable workman-like outfit of black trousers, long leather riding boots, a wide leather belt buckled around my waist and topped off with a crisp snowy white shirt. The long boots helped protect from possible snake bites.

Taking the reptiles from their crates, I'd let them slither around on the floor of the pit as the viewing area filled with paying customers. I would then lower myself into the pit to handle the serpents and demonstrate how to milk a poisonous snake of its venom.

Over the years we collected death adders, tiger snakes and a variety from the brown snake family – including the deadliest of all, the eastern common brown – followed by the king brown, scaly back brown, copperheads and the Western Australia dugite. On rare occasions, we had the vicious and deadly Queensland taipan, which has the longest fangs of any Australian snake. Added to these were the less deadly red-bellied blacks, tree snakes and the bandy-bandy.

The bandy-bandy is a beautiful snake with black-and-white stripes running around the length of its long, thin body. I often used this snake to demonstrate the flexibility of a snake's body, by tying it into a knot and letting it slowly unravel as it lay on my open palms. We also showed some lizards such as goannas, blue tongues, frill-necked and the thorny devils, plus a number of the huge constricting reptiles like carpet snakes and other pythons.

In all the years that we had the snake show, the only bite I ever had was from a goanna. We were out hunting in bushland when I sighted this great 3-foot-long goanna. As I tussled with it, it got me, clamping its jaws around my left hand. The pain was excruciating. A sledgehammer to the head would not hurt anywhere near as much. Still, he didn't beat me. I ended up bagging the little blighter.

Mick always went with me when hunting snakes. As much as he feared these creatures, he feared for my safety more. His job was to carry the bags that could hold two or three snakes. He could spot a snake from 20 feet, well back from a snake strike. On spying one he would freeze and point while yelling, 'Snake!'

Bagging the snakes was easy. Finding them (even with Mick's eagle eyes) was something else. Snakes have no eardrums, but they can feel a vibration in the ground. So we'd hunt along waterways, aware that wherever water lay, there was less vibration. Farmers' sheds and around hay and grain stores were also good spots. Once sighted, it was only a matter of quickly scooping the snake up using a hooked metal rod or pinning stick.

Laurie Neville, a young man we both knew well, approached us to work in the snake show. Laurie was from an old-time family of vaudeville show people and wanted to get into a show of his own. His knowledge of reptiles was quite remarkable. He was soon an assistant in the show and taking on all the bush work to replenish the snakes, while helping out in our outfit wherever else he was needed. Laurie couldn't have turned up at a better time, as child number four was on the way. Baby Warren entered this world in October 1963.

I'd now had four children in six years. I felt lucky to have two wonderful girls on the staff from the Wanda illusion show to help me, but I still had a hell of a workload. And where was I to put the new baby in our 22-foot caravan? After some thought, I built a large sliding drawer type of cot for little Warren to sleep in. This fitted perfectly under our bed when not in use. Or at least, it did until Mick noticed the drawer open one evening and without thinking shoved it shut with his foot – not noticing Warren all snuggled up, fast asleep inside. A new cot was swiftly built above the foot of our bed, complete with a safety rail!

With the gaming stalls doing well and the snake show functioning perfectly with Laurie at the helm, everything was running great. Best of all, I was only needed on rare occasions. We decided this was the perfect time to branch out yet again. We were going to move into burlesque. With the general public now clamouring for more 'adult' shows, the more innocent illusion-type shows were getting old hat. We would open a strip-and-tease show or, in our parlance, 'a leg-and-belly show'.

During the Christmas break of 1963, we bought a large canvas tent and hired another girl to perform as a tease dancer, while Sandie and Colleen trained as support dancers. New girl Dianne had the cheekiest grin. I got to work on new pictorial banners while Mick worked with Laurie and another man on our staff to make the burlesque act possible.

There were costumes to organise and intensive training to be had, but finally we were ready. Our first burlesque performance was held at the New Year's Day Rodeo in the Victorian town of Myrtleford, between Wangaratta and Bright.

It had been quite a few years since I had spruiked on a line-up board outside a sideshow tent. With all the show-goers' eyes on you, it was quite different to spruiking in the confines of a ticket box. Not that it was the general public that I was concerned with. It was our opposition.

With four other illusion and freak shows at the Myrtleford Rodeo, plus our snake show, the competition was fierce. With ours being the only leg-and-belly line-up show, my heart was pounding. If I lined up at the wrong time (just as the other spruikers were turning the public into their tents), they would gang up by turning their speakers directly onto me, making it impossible for the public to listen to my spiel. Or worse still, if the boxing tent started to belt their drums, we would be out of business before we'd even started. Yes, we were all a community who'd help each other out. But when it was show time, it was show time. Business was business.

So there I was, standing just inside the door of our tent in a lather of sweat, with the girls just as bad, ready to go onto the line-up board. This was their first time performing as artistic dancing girls. Mick, feeling the tension all round, said, 'Hold on, luv. I'll get you a cuppa to calm your nerves.'

A minute later, he was back carrying four mugs. 'Right, get this into yous.'

With that, we all up-ended our mugs to swallow an unexpected shot of straight whiskey! From that moment on, we never looked back, and I never again needed a shot of whiskey before the big show.

Generally, the girls would run the show inside, with me spruiking and doing one act. One of those acts was my performance as a psychic medium, as taught to me by Australia's leading country singer, Tex Morton. Tex, who had become a good friend over the years, had used this performance in many of his shows around the world.

The opening and the order of each 20-minute performance of the burlesque show was ably assisted by Sandie who, with microphone in hand, would introduce the psychic medium, Madam Zarina. 'By using only the power of her mind, she will inform you of your past, present and future.'

Madam Zarina (me), decked out in a full-length gown of many colours with a definite Far Eastern flavour, walked out onto the stage from the curtained backdrop. Sandie then invited a young man from the audience to come up onto the stage and blindfold Madam Zarina.

Sitting Madam on a swivel chair in the middle of the stage, the young man placed a 2-shilling coin on each eye, which was held in place with a sticking plaster. A folded sheet of newspaper was then placed over the eyes, with a black cloth tied over the lot. Madam Zarina, totally blindfolded, was now turned to face the curtained backdrop, away from the audience.

Sandie walked along the front row, at times touching one or another of the public as she asked Madam various questions such as: 'Madam Zarina, can you tell me if this is a man or a woman I am touching?'

Madam would answer without hesitation. 'That is a lady.' If it was a child, Madam would say whether it was a boy or a girl. Of course, we would add a bit of humour, such as when a small boy was chosen, I would be asked if he was married or single and how many children he had. The questions would continue right around the rows of people. Madam would even be asked to describe what certain audience members were wearing.

By this point, the audience was either completely awed by the questions or in fits of laughter at the absurdity of it all. Sandie, toward the end of the performance, would ask for the assistance of a young man to gather several articles from the people in the audience and place them on a tray (coin, watch, handkerchief, comb, lipstick and so on). Returning to the stage, Sandie asked the young man to turn the chair once again toward the audience and place the tray on Madam's lap, so the audience had a perfect view of the contents of the tray. With blindfold still firmly in place, Madam would then perform her grand finale. Sandie used a long stick to point to various articles on the tray. 'Madam, can you tell me what I am touching now?'

I gave the correct answer every time. How did I do it? Well, that's for Madam Zarina to know and for you to never find out!

After my psychic act, I'd scoot out the front and entice more of the public to line up for the next show. Meanwhile, inside, Colleen (renamed 'Mallarme') would perform the belly-bumping dance of a very naughty hula-hula, publicised as 'coming direct from the South Sea Islands'. She'd wriggle her hips and get cheeky with all the boys. The trick with these shows was to include the audience in the act, but only so far!

The final act was performed by Dianne, the new girl with the show, dancing under the name of 'Suzette-La-Gay'. My spruiking went something like this: 'Our beautiful Suzette-La-Gay, from gay Paree, will be slowly removing her veils in the exotic Dance of the Seven Veils, until only one veil remains. You certainly won't be writing home to your mother about this one!'

Sure enough, moving in time to tantalising music, this lovely dancer removed veil after veil as she twirled, teasing the young men with her sultry, flowing movements until finally, there was only one veil left. By this time the audience was yelling, whistling and clapping wildly. The finale to this daring performance occurred just as the stage curtain was closing and Suzette gave the audience a naughty glimpse of her bare bot as she flicked through the curtain. Dropping the final veil. Ooh la la! Remember, these were the days when women out in public were certainly not flashing much flesh! In fact, any bare boobs and we would have been charged. Burlesque was theatrical and big on suggestion.

As the people left the marquee, announcer Sandie informed them that Madam Zarina was available for private sittings after the final show of the day. These sittings were very well patronised and another source of revenue.

Even during these successful years, the showie life could prove cruel. But always, the resilience of my people shone through. I will never forget the time I was approached at Victoria's Geelong show by Marie Short. A woman well into her seventies, Marie was a sideshow spruiker of some repute –rough, tough and not one for any nonsense. She ran her show with an iron fist and would work from early morning right through until late at night on the line-up board on the outside of her tent. While she was cajoling her captive audience into entering her show tent, she would tell more furphies than any other spruiker and get away with it. In fact, her audience loved it when she openly stated that she was the world's greatest liar.

But the night she came to see me it was clear she had a big problem. The main girl who worked for her had done a 'moonlight flit' – that is, she had taken off without notice. Marie's show was called 'The Burning of a Beautiful Virgin Named Desiree' – and now she had no Desiree.

'What will I do?' Marie asked me. Before I could answer, she asked if I could help her out by lending her one of my dancers. Overhearing this, my dancing girls made a fast exit, stating that they had to help Mick. My brain started to work overtime. Finally, I came up with a solution. I suggested she go and see the town's local priest, as he would know if there was a young woman who would be keen to perform in a sideshow tent to earn a quid.

Later in the day, Mick noticed Marie's show was in full swing. We were having a short break, so we walked down the line of tent shows to where Marie was spruiking, telling all and sundry about the wonders they would see. We wanted to see who she had managed to get to help her out. Maybe she'd followed my advice.

'Ladies and gentlemen,' Marie was saying loudly, 'on the inside of this huge marquee we will present for your edification a remarkable wonder of our age. You will see a beautiful virgin we have named "Desiree" in all her naked beauty, being burnt alive before your very eyes. Come one, come all. Don't miss this wonder of the age.'

On and on Marie spruiked, extolling the unbelievable sights they were about to see, collecting their money as they went in.

Mick and I slipped inside, curious about this new Desiree. Marie entered to announce that the show was about to begin. The stage curtains were drawn back to reveal a huge metal coffin on a high bench, with a flaming torch mounted on one end.

Marie announced in dramatic tones: 'Ladies and gentlemen, before we start the show, I would ask all the people inside this marquee to make me a promise that what is about to be revealed here today shall remain a secret, that you on your oath you will never tell your friends. Let them pay their admission at the ticket box as you have today. And now, I present to you, The Virgin Desiree.'

With a deep curtsy, Marie swung around from the coffin as the back curtains drew open. The patrons watched with bated breaths as Desiree was slowly revealed to be … a brand-new straw broom (yes, a virgin broom).

Marie tossed the broom into the metal coffin and slathered it with lighter fluid. She then snatched up the burning torch. BOOM! The virgin broom was quickly devoured by flames, and Desiree was no more. The audience reacted with applause, whistles and cheers. Everyone around us was laughing about how they would con their mates to see this show.

In that moment, I realised I was fortunate in seeing a consummate sideshow spruiker continue to operate her show in the face of adversity. Marie jam-packed every performance throughout the Geelong show; and the hardware stores had a field day, selling every 'virgin' straw broom in stock.

Over the next few years, we ran a variety of successful sideshows. We introduced the fabulous Shim Sham Shimmy jitter bug dance at all the major shows, adding ballet dancers to our troupe. This idea came from my childhood with the vaudeville tent shows.

Mick, who was always in the background taking care of the vehicles, swapped a surplus truck and gaming stalls for a beaut caravan for the girls, which we towed behind the station wagon. It had two double bunks at one end, a mountain of cupboards and a tiny little kitchen. But the girls rarely used the kitchen as they still ate with us in the cookhouse tent, along with Laurie Neville and his offsider, Peter, who now assisted him in the snake show.

It was during this time that I learnt I was once again pregnant. Mick was so pleased to learn I was pregnant with baby number five that he made this brilliant comment: 'Oh no! Not another one!'

Our fifth child, Ashley, was born in August 1965. I'd basically been pregnant for ten years, with my babies born at whichever town we happened to be showing in.

On travel days, Mick and I shared the kids between us, making up beds on the floors of both trucks. I always had the baby as I was the only person equipped to feed it.

These were very much the days when the extended showie family spent the hours, days and years together. We all cared for each other. When I'd put my head out the caravan door and call 'Mick, cuppa made!', you could hear the echo of voices calling, 'Mick, cuppa made!' The echo would return, 'On my way, luv!' He would always arrive with a mate or two, or more, all wanting a cuppa.

Sometimes my shout from the caravan door would be, 'Has anyone seen Gary?' The echo would come back from one camp to the next, until eventually I would hear something like, 'He's helping Joe set up the merry-go-round!'

'Well, tell him to get back here as he's got his own work to do!'

Our kids were rarely out of sight. Each was under the watchful surveillance of the parents, the other showfolk and the long-time staff, all of whom had made this lifestyle theirs into perpetuity. This was our home; this was our life.

It was not unusual to find a few extra kids who had decided to have a feed or had just come to play. By evening you would hear the mothers doing a roll call to be sure there were no extras.

I remember one time when all my kids went down with the flu. I wasn't too good myself and was running a fever. It was time for their medicine – a banana-flavoured syrup. Calling all my kids, I started dishing out this nice-tasting medicine. In the rush, there seemed to be a lot of open mouths. When I did a head count, I realised I had dosed my own kids along with all the other show kids as well!

Show nights were difficult when the kids were little. You would have to bed them down under your stall counter or on the ticket box floor. It was just as well they were used to sleeping through the noise of drums and ringing bells from the boxing tent, the roar of the motor bikes from the Globe of Death, the spruikers announcing the wonderful virtues of the Polynesian dancing girls, or 'Electros the Electrified Lady', who was about to have 20,000 volts of electricity pass through her body. Overlaying all this was the high-pitched music from a dozen different rides, all playing a different tune. But wait, there was more! Add in the screams of the excited teenagers and the parents yelling to control their smaller children who had filled their tummies with fairy floss, Dagwood dogs and donuts.

Sandie, Colleen and Dianne were a great help to me with the kids. However, there was a new girl we took on, Rita, who was a problem from the first day. She was a habitual swearer. I don't think she even realised she was doing it. After a few weeks in her company, the other girls and my kids had started copying Rita, using all sorts of foul language. Something had to be done.

I put it to Rita that she stop swearing. I tried speaking to the girls and even docking their wages. Nothing worked. In desperation, I suggested to all the girls that they could break the habit if they used the correct lingo. For instance, instead of 'bastard', say 'illegitimate'. And instead of 'You're a f---ing c---', you say 'You're an intercourse woman's pussy!' There were other swear words that they swapped for more proper English as well, often amidst hysterical laughter. Well, it worked! As a team, they pulled each other up, with one correcting the other. And the swearing stopped.

Chapter 18

Zarack the Yogi Man

1965–1968

Some time in the mid-60s, we were in outback Queensland, setting up for the Winton Rodeo, when this chap approached Mick looking for a job. He was having a rough trot. His name was Robert (Bob) Laffey. A tall, muscular man, he had hoped to meet up with the sideshow man Fred Duffy, who he had worked with previously. As it turned out, Fred's truck had broken down and he wouldn't arrive for at least a week. Now Bob was desperate for any type of work.

Ever the hospitable showies, we invited Bob to join up with us. What was one more mouth to feed? You should have seen the relief on his face. Then, before we knew it, Bob was introducing us to his wife, Eileen, plus two little boys and a baby girl! They had barely eaten for days and were camped in their rusting old car near the cattle pens on the rodeo grounds.

Laurie, our snake man, took matters into his own hands. He

moved out of his little caravan and let Bob, Eileen and their three beautiful kids move in.

Bob and his mob could not have arrived at a better time for us. It turned out that Eileen was a pretty good cook. And when the rodeo kicked off, we discovered that Bob was exceptionally good on a microphone. He could 'drag a pitch' (gather a group of listeners) with the utmost ease. For me in particular, Bob and his wife were a godsend. I desperately needed a break. So, just as his wife took over the cooking, Bob took over a good deal of the spruiking.

We soon discovered that Bob had another hidden talent for pulling a crowd. As 'The Human Pin Cushion', he was the ideal warm-up for our burlesque show.

Speaking into the microphone while scratching a large circle on the ground in front of the line-up board, Bob would begin by cajoling the gathering crowd to move in closer. 'I'm going to thrill and amaze you at no cost whatsoever. What you are about to see is completely free of charge!'

After several minutes of this patter, he had a huge crowd. He would then announce, 'Ladies and gentlemen, watch closely as I am going to take this length of common old fencing wire and push it right through the muscle of my arm – in one side and out through the other.'

The audience would gasp as Bob would then shove the wire through the flesh and muscle of his arm. As the blood would gush, Bob would then hand me the microphone. This was my signal to bring out the girls, using the old show terminology of 'Figgarlarpa', meaning 'Hurry girls, it's show time.'

As the girls climbed onto the platform, wearing ankle-length cloaks complete with hoods and masks, I explained that they were beautiful beyond belief. 'For that reason, until they are back inside the marquee, they will have to remain covered, as there is a possibility that some of you will be blinded by their sheer beauty. So, buy your tickets now to see the daring, exotically beautiful dancing girls. They will make your shirt run up and down your back like a venetian blind.'

On filling the tent with our now bedazzled audience, the girls started their half-hour performance. For the rest of the day, we spruiked Bob's sure-fire fencing-wire crowd-pleaser. All the while, I was mentally putting together a brand-new show, with Bob centre stage.

After our outback run, we headed back to Brisbane to sort out the gear we needed for this new act, which we would debut on the New South Wales show run. We would call our new sideshow 'Zarack the Yogi Man'.

The title for our show came from Fred Duffy, who told us back in Winton that 'Zarack' was the name he had first used when he came into the business. He was something of a mystery himself, old Fred Duffy. He turned up some time in the 1950s as a spruiker on one of the girlie shows. In a gravelly voice, he would give a vibrant and most graphic account of the wonderful virtues of the lovely ladies. A gregarious man, always with a huge smile and a laugh, he was everyone's friend, often shouting drinks for his mates at the public bar on show day. I wouldn't say that he was the world's best spruiker, but he had a presence about him that captivated his audience.

When introducing the striptease artists, Fred would often remove from a bag a live carpet snake, using the snake to draw more attention to his spiel. It worked! Towards the end of the day, Fred would announce, 'This is the final show of the day! It is the late, late, late, late, late show. So, hurry, hurry, it's where she will take it all off … stripping to the bare skin that God gave her. She will make the old feel young and the young feel like spring chickens.' By repeating this spiel over and over again, Fred would fill the tent to capacity.

(Ten years later, working alongside us at the Darwin show, Fred was bitten by his pet snake. The ambulance rushed him to hospital, but he died within hours. There were plenty of rumours as to why he died. Was he given the wrong medication? Not likely. Did he have a heart attack? A lot more likely. But the fact remained: Fred was gone. Just as he came in with flair, he left the same way.)

For our new Zarack show, I painted a set of banners. With these banners as a backdrop outside the tent, Bob could stride the line-up platform, spruiking the wonders that would be shown inside.

This would be a very compact one-man show, with Bob both spruiker and star of the show, while Eileen sold the tickets. I made Bob an outfit to wear, which consisted of smart tailored black trousers, highly polished dress shoes, a bare chest and a floor-length, beautifully embroidered silver and blue brocaded cape. Bob really looked the part.

By the time we arrived in Perth for the show, Bob's performance as Zarack was so powerful that we could be sure of at least one customer passing out in shock, horror or both in every performance. With his reputation preceding him, this was the best publicity Bob could get, and he was always adding more shocking stunts to his repertoire, beyond the original wire stabbing act.

With as many as 100 people jammed into his tent, 'Zarack' would begin his show by selecting a white mouse from a glass case full of the sweet, little darlings. With no warning, he would then bite the head right off the tiny creature. At this stage, we could be sure of at least one customer passing out.

Following this rather gruesome opening, and with blood running down his chin, Bob went into a self-induced hypnotic trance and proceeded to push pins and needles into various parts of his body, taking on the appearance of a huge pin cushion. While some people started leaving the tent rather hurriedly, the majority stayed, transfixed.

Finally, Bob invited a member of the audience to throw a dart into his bare chest. Sometimes there was a delay as nobody dared raise their trembling hand, but eventually a contender would step into the arena.

Bob would prepare by moving to the rear of his small stage and checking that there was no one nearby who might accidently be speared by a stray dart. He then invited the dart thrower to take aim and throw as hard as he could, right into the middle of Bob's chest. The thrower would often be a bit wary at first, tossing the dart so softly that it bounced off Bob's chest. With Bob's encouragement, the second dart invariably broke the skin a bit. By now, Bob was teasing and challenging them, 'Is that the best you can do?' The third dart then plunged into his bare chest, and stayed there. And inevitably, another member of the audience would crumple in shock.

Amid the gasps, Bob would calmly pull the dart from his chest, leaving a trickle of blood. Thanking everyone for coming, he would inform them that there would be another show within a half hour. 'And please, tell your friends so they can come and be attended to … completely free of charge by our resident ambulance!' It was true. We did have an ambulance on hand, for the audience members who fainted, not Bob. Sometimes five or six people passed out at his performance. We kept that ambulance busy. The act took no longer than ten minutes, but the show outside lasted a lot longer, with the ambulance making full use of the line-up platform for people to sit on as they were being treated.

(I should point out that Bob didn't really bite the head off the mouse. He palmed it in his large hands, while biting down on a blood capsule.)

Once again, we were on a winner. It's not what you see; it's what you believe you see. And as for the those darts … I'll leave that to your imagination.

We knew that Zarack's fame had spread far and wide when a police car pulled up outside the show one day. (I could tell you which city and state this took place in, but for reasons that will soon become clear, I'd better not.) Out stepped none other than the Chief of Police. Apparently, he had heard all the reports of our gruesome and shocking act. So he decided to turn up in person, to shut us down.

'Listen here, you can't have someone getting darts thrown at them. It's not legal,' he said.

'You show me in the legislation where this is illegal,' I retorted. 'There's nothing there about not throwing darts into people.' You should have seen the look on his face. 'Anyway, have you seen the show?'

'No, I don't want to,' he said.

'Really? So, you're prepared to close us down without even seeing what you're closing down?'

Pause.

'I suggest you watch the next performance,' I said. 'It's on the house. Then you can make an informed decision.'

With that, I shoved him inside the tent. 'It's only a 10-minute show. You'll be okay.' He just nodded.

First, it was off with the mouse's head. Well, the police chief didn't seem too keen on that, but he stayed put. Mind you, I noticed him going a little white. 'You all right?' I asked.

'Sure. Of course. I'm a trained police officer,' he replied, squaring up his uniformed shoulders.

Then along came that the third dart, straight into Bob's chest. Well, that copper went right over in a faint, landing on the floor with a thud.

He came around after a few seconds. 'You all right?' I asked again.

'What happened?' he asked, as he hauled himself up.

'Well, you keeled right over. And I think you better leave the tent as soon as possible because the newspaper fellow saw it all and is going to get the photographer to take your photo. You're going to be on the front page.'

Well, did he hightail it out of there quick smart. And that was the last we saw of him.

Zarack the Yogi Man turned out to be the best one-man show we ever had.

During the time that Bob and his family travelled with us, he proved to be a most caring man, always treating me and Mick with the highest regard. All our kids got on well together, even the smallest of ours, whom Eileen had taken on herself to leave me more time for my work.

Within the first year, Bob managed to fix up his old car and buy his own caravan. In 1967, now financially well-off, Bob decided to give the shows away. His wife wanted to settle back near her family in Gympie. At the Charleville show, we held a big going-away party to wish them well.

Some years later, we learnt of Bob's tragic death, in a caravan fire on their property. The strange thing is that Bob had forecast his own death. He often stated that he would die by fire. He was most adamant about this. RIP Bob 'Zarack' Laffey.

Chapter 19

Crash, Bang, Boom

Late 1969

After closing the Zarack show, we reduced our convoy to two buses and a trailer for the show gear. We also changed the old station wagon for a heavy-duty Ford ute, suitable for towing Laurie's caravan.

Returning to Brisbane for a short spell, we figured one more bus for ourselves would do the trick. So Mick went shopping for a second-hand bus at an auction sale. And lucky me, I would have the job of fitting out the new bus.

Well, instead of a little bus, home Mick came with a huge, interstate coach that I swear was double the size of the buses we had. It was equipped with long-range fuel tanks and massive, dust-proof storage lockers underneath.

My wonderful husband Mick wasn't too good with the power tools. But he did have other advantages, not least being the fact that he served me up a hot breakfast in bed every morning. (And he did so for most of our fifty years together.) There was also no doubt that he was one of the greatest dads in the world; just ask any of his kids.

So, I was the handywoman. While we did have a professional cabinetmaker fit out a small kitchen in the centre of the bus, as we were on a tight schedule, the rest of the job was naturally up to me. I built a bathroom in the rear with a shower, vanity and small portable toilet. The toilet was a brand-new idea for those days. Our bed with storage drawers underneath was next, with a very compact wardrobe and dressing table completing the room. The next room alongside the rear door was the kitchenette and a dining area with built-in storage seats and table. The front room, which also had a an entry door and the driver's seat, was the lounge and children's room. The kids' beds doubled as lounge seats during the day and was where they could all do their correspondence lessons. At night, the backrests folded up to form double bunks, with drawers underneath. This gave our kids four comfortable beds. A small mobile bunk was Ashley's bed as he was still only a toddler, and overhead lockers built above all the windows around the bus gave plenty of storage space.

The good thing about our big new bus was that during night travel, I could put the kids into their beds (completely locked in with safety rails), where they would drift off to sleep in one town then wake up to a brand-new backyard in another town.

Behind the bus we towed our heavy-duty 24-foot trailer full of show equipment which, when unloaded, gave us a mobile stage to use in the tent. Another of Mick's ideas.

I had a time-saving idea of my own, too. Before we set off, I would fill a metal rubbish bin with soapy water and our dirty laundry, then sit it in the rear door compartment of the bus. On arrival at our next campsite, the clothes were well and truly vibrated clean, only needing rinsing and hanging to dry!

While on the subject of laundry, an event happened back in the early 60s, when washing machines first came on the market. Mick arrived home with a surprise gift for me. It was a very modern super-duper washing machine named 'Sapphire Turner'. It was huge and heavy and took two men to lift from the truck to set up alongside our caravan. After unloading, a fair crowd of show people gathered to view this wondrous machine. Mick set to running out an extension lead to plug into the machine while a couple of the men immediately bucketed water to fill the round inner tub of the machine.

After placing soiled clothes and soap powder in, amid lots of advice from the women and kids who had gathered round, we finally had the machine running. Swoosh, swoosh, it went, turning first one way then the other. Some of the onlookers were edging back as the machine started to jerk about on the slightly sloped ground. Then the machine took off, juddering off down the paddock. The men were grabbing and yelling at it to stop, soapy water bubbling out all over them as it gathered speed. The women and kids were in the middle of this melee when, as suddenly as it had started, it stopped. The Sapphire Turner, with a mind of its own, had run out of electric lead and had unplugged itself. After this, the machine was bolted firmly to the floor of the truck, where it happily resided for some years, well off uneven ground.

With the 1969 Darwin show all done, we prepared for the long haul to Perth. With five weeks to spare until the Perth show, we were thankful there was no rush. We were fully aware that the roads could be extremely bad. But the whole family was looking forward to seeing this part of the country, especially as we would stop off first in Broome to see firsthand the pearling industry that we had heard so much about.

Before leaving Darwin, we had the vehicles fully serviced, with new tyres put on the buses. With plenty of water and food on board, we were all set. Also, having hired a new chap named Peter to drive the ute and work with Laurie on the snake show, I wasn't required as a driver. This meant I had the rare chance to travel with Mick. I could stretch out and catch up on some much-needed rest, while the kids could move around in the bus (in the days before seat belts were compulsory).

Heading for Kununurra, the corrugations in the road made for exhausting driving. It was essential to maintain a speed between twenty and thirty miles per hour. At that rate, we mostly skimmed over the top of the road; any less and we'd be driving in and out of the ruts that were so deep the constant shaking would rattle your teeth right out of your gums.

After Kununurra, our next break was the tiny township of Wyndham, at the very top of Western Australia. From there on, things changed. I don't know which was worse – the bulldust that had built up on both sides of the road or the deep corrugations. It became impossible to maintain a steady speed. By the time we reached Fitzroy Crossing, our next overnight stop, I'll swear that no bucking bronco had ever left me as thoroughly shaken up.

At the 'Fitz', we were pleased to meet up with fellow showman Slim Geesman and his wife Edna, who made us very welcome. Sitting around the campfire that night, Slim told us he was headed for the Broome Rodeo but on the way planned to stop off at Derby to run a two-day carnival there. After Broome, he would take his time as he headed down for the Perth Show. If we liked, we were welcome to travel along with him.

We took him up on his offer. Slim and Edna were the salt of the earth, and very hard workers. With their little carnival, they showed at the missions and small back country towns across South Australia, the Northern Territory and Western Australia. They worked this vast area year after year. Little did we know, their friendship would soon prove essential.

The next day was Mick's forty-fifth birthday: 6 August 1969. What a mongrel of a milestone it would prove to be.

We'd hit the road very early in the morning to beat the heat. Slim's outfit had headed off even earlier, travelling a good hour ahead of us, so he could mark out sites on the carnival grounds at Derby for the extra camps.

It was 8am. We were chatting away about our Perth plans as we came out of one of the many gullies along the narrow, rutted road, when a huge semi-trailer loomed out of a dust cloud. It was hurtling straight at us, on our side of the road! Mick's instincts kicked in and he wrenched the wheel hard, hitting the soft embankment of dust on his left. Suddenly we were airborne. We spun around in a complete circle, facing back the way we had come. With an almighty crash, we came to a mind-jarring stop, landing astride the gully we had just driven through. The front wheels of the bus were buried deep in the far embankment, with the rear straddling the opposite bank. The trailer had been wrenched completely off, with all our equipment scattered, torn and broken across the dusty terrain.

Of the semi there was no sign. With all the dust, he probably didn't even know we had crashed. I'd been thrown the length of the lounge. Landing in a tangled heap in the front stairwell compartment, I was unable to move, the door of the bus having been torn from its hinges and now wrapped around me.

I remember screaming and yelling for the kids. Where were they? Were they okay?

After struggling to extract himself from the mangled driver's seat, Mick somehow squirmed out of the narrow driver's window and jumped down into the crevice below. He raced to the back of the bus to cut the engine and avoid an explosion. Then he dragged the door off me. With massive relief, he found that baby Ashley was unhurt. The bub had skidded off his sister's bunk on a big, soft cushion, into the stairwell, with me landing alongside. Until this moment, I'd had no idea he was there – he was very quiet, just looking around with a big smile on his face. The little bugger thought it was great fun!

Mick turned his attention to the other kids. Though not badly hurt, they were crying in fear and shock at their world turned topsy-turvy. What a bastard of a birthday. One never to be forgotten.

Three station hands working on fences nearby had heard the thunderous crash and came galloping up on their horses. One of them left to get help from the nearby township of Camballin.

Our other bus turned up a short time later. Laurie, with the three dancing girls, had been keeping well back out of our dust and had passed the semi back along the road. All the while, the girls comforted and looked after the kids. I don't know what we would have done without Laurie and those wonderful young women. They were not only the backbone of our business; they were like our own flesh and blood. They had travelled with us for years, referring to us as Mum and Dad and often helping out with the kids' school lessons (even though most of the time the correspondence school lessons would be lost somewhere in the postal system!).

Meanwhile, the bush telegraph did what it did best. Word went out about our smash and, no doubt, the fact that we had three beautiful dancing girls travelling with us. By nightfall, half the population of not only Camballin but also Derby turned up to help us, offering up accommodation until we could sort ourselves out.

By the following afternoon, the bus had been dragged into Camballin, where a mechanic declared it a write-off. The tail shaft had speared right through the differential. There was substantial damage to the body, and the luggage locker, packed with our amplifiers and other sound gear, was smashed to bits. Strangely enough, all the building I had done had stood up well except for the professionally built kitchenette, which was torn to pieces. What really hurt was that we lost all our family photos (which is why there are limited photos of some of the years I share in this book). You see, some locals (I won't say who) raided the crash site and took off with whatever they could find.

As for us, I seemed to have copped the most battering and bruising. And not just to my body. This time, I felt my mind was being battered. How much could a woman take?

A few days later, after the men had done what repairs they could to the trailer, and loaded it up with what could be salvaged, we limped on to the carnival in Derby in what vehicles we had left. (Laurie's offsider, Peter, had decided that as our dancers wouldn't have anything to do with him, he would move onto greener pastures at the mines.)

In the meantime, I contacted our insurance company to put in a claim. We were told that our bus had bald tyres, which had caused the smash. Even when I produced receipts for the service and new tyres, I still couldn't convince them. To cut a long story short, we were wiped by the insurance company. We were gutted. Little did we know that we could have put this in the hands of the law courts. Our lack of education unfortunately cost us dearly.

Everything we'd worked so hard for had bitten the dust in that one big crash. Our show banners were ripped to bits, and our main tent was in bad shape. We didn't have the machinery or material to repair it. As if that wasn't enough, all our sound systems were ruined. It looked like we were out of business.

Even the Showman's Guild of Australia refused to help us. We were offered no assistance from the Benevolence Fund, into which all show people pay a compulsory sum each year, along with our normal guild fees. Their reasoning was that the funds were only to be used in the case of a funeral.

The only support we were getting was from dear ol' Slim and Edna. They allowed our three beautiful young ladies to work their stalls at the carnival, and Edna stepped in to help with our kids. With no children of her own, she became a surrogate mother to mine and spoiled them rotten. Bless her, because I just wasn't coping.

By the time we moved from Derby to Broome, where we were to give Slim a hand setting up his carnival gear, I was well and truly depressed. I knew I was overworking and overwrought, but what could I do?

Finally, I lost the plot, completely. I broke down. The tears wouldn't stop. The littlest thing would set me off. It was as if the stuffing had been punched out of me. I felt like I was shattered into a million tiny pieces. I ended up, literally, a heap on the floor.

Mick picked me up in his strong arms and took me to the bush hospital in Broome. I was diagnosed as having a nervous collapse. Bustled into the Royal Flying Doctor plane, I was taken to Perth, as the Broome doctor didn't have the expertise to treat me.

In Perth, I was assessed at the Claremont Mental Hospital (the same place where Mick had been treated for severe depression years before). It was noted that I was excessively underweight, weighing only 6 stone 2 lb (39 kilograms), and suffering from malnutrition.

I was a skeleton. The doctor told me, 'You are a walking dead woman.' He didn't need to tell me. I felt it.

Back in Broome, Mick felt he was going to lose me forever. He was blaming himself for all the years of stress I had been through, for failing to notice that after cooking and dishing up for everyone, I often forgot to feed myself. I couldn't remember the last time I sat down and ate a meal. I had been the glue holding everything together, but now I had come unstuck.

The treatment was surprisingly simple and worked very quickly: anti-depressants and total bed rest, with a potent diet. From memory, this consisted of a two-litre jug of pure liquid glucose and high-energy vitamins that I had to drink twice a day, with a nurse to assist me. I was told by one of the nurses that this same treatment was most effective on soldiers released from concentration camps following World War II. Believe me, I needed that nurse! The first couple of mouthfuls were okay, but then the fun began as the nurse held the glass to my mouth. Choking, gagging and spluttering, I was force-fed this atrocious concoction of liquid glucose. I was told by the doctors that if I didn't drink the lot, I would have only three months left to live.

I was only thirty-three years old. I had fitted so much into my life. Was this where I wanted to finish up – at the gates of the ward for the mentally ill, behind locked doors? During this time, and after several talks with the wonderful nursing staff and doctors, I eventually stopped crying and started to get my act into gear, to ready myself for the next ride on the hurdy-gurdy of my life.

After three weeks I was back on my feet. I regained a fair amount of energy and put on some weight. But the doctors warned me not to do any exercise, otherwise I would lose a lot of this weight once I left hospital and started to move around. I had to maintain a high-protein diet, as it could take many months to reach my normal weight of 8 stone 7lbs. So, I ate a lot of cheese and eggs (and I hate eggs), and basically anything with protein in it (except meat). I could still have my old life, but it had to be more regulated, with a healthy balance of work, rest and play. I would have to learn to delegate some of the workload and not do it all myself.

Mick, meanwhile, was having his own dramas in my absence.

After packing me off to Perth by plane, he had once again taken to the road. He wanted to reach Perth as quickly as possible to be with me. The children were sharing the small bus with the dancers, and Mick was sleeping in the great outdoors with a knapsack. From what was once a very well-organised show outfit, our family was now back to where we had started: on the bones of our arse. Well, I was lying on mine in a hospital bed.

Trouble struck again about 30 miles south of Port Hedland, when Shayne started to scream in pain. She'd had stomach pains for some time and now needed a doctor. Back they went to Port Hedland. There, Shayne was found to be suffering with acute appendicitis and was operated on the next day.

After a week in hospital, Shayne was released, all fit and well. It's strange how certain illnesses seem to strike in the same family. First, my brother, then me and now my daughter. All suffering with the same complaint! Of course, I was unaware of all this until I returned home. They didn't want to worry me.

When I was finally ready to leave Claremont Hospital, my husband and children were still on the road to Perth. So I went to stay with my in-laws, Jim and Thelma, Mick's wonderful brother and sister-in-law.

With Jim's help, I arranged for the hire of two tents and a sound system, plus a caravan large enough for our family.

Poor Mick didn't arrive until the night before the Perth show's opening. He and his bedraggled charges had endured blown tires, engine problems and a broken axle on what was left of the trailer. By the time he staggered in, Mick had only a couple of shilling coins (20¢) left in his pocket. It had been one hell of an experience. We vowed never to travel that way again, or at least not until the powers that be had graded the roads properly!

By the time the kids were cuddled, fed and tucked into their beds in the rented caravan, and everyone else had been given a good home-cooked meal, it was a late night. But at least we were set up. As long as the outside of our show looked shipshape, it would be okay with the show society, even if we weren't ready with the inside. Needless to say, we opened at the Perth show pretty well worn out.

None of this would have been possible without the physical and monetary assistance of Mick's family. Thanks to them, the dancers had their costumes ready for the show and the hired caravan, the girls' bus and Laurie's caravan were all set up out the back of the tent.

With gratitude and relief, we watched our little kids take off to find their mates – the Western Australian show kids whose families only worked in this state – who they hadn't seen for a full year.

Then Laurie came to talk to us about his plans. With his caravan a write-off, shaken to death on the atrocious roads, he'd decided it was time to give away the snakes. He would head north and find work at the mines after the Perth show.

Well, that was it; no more Laurie or snakes. I had been warned by the doctors to take it easy, so we were lucky enough to hire another spruiker who could set up the pitch on show days. Mick was in charge of the ticket box, while the kids made sure I stuck to my diet.

After the Perth show, it was time to take stock of the mess we were in. We had lost so much equipment, including our home on wheels. While we pondered our next move, we rented a partly furnished house in the suburb of Leederville. It was a nice place, but very crowded with our five kids and the three girls.

It was here that we prepared for more goodbyes. We asked our beloved dancing girls if they would like to return home to their families, with all fares paid plus a big bonus for their long service. Dianne reluctantly agreed, but Sandy and Colleen both refused to leave. They felt we were their family. (It was many years later that I ran into Dianne at the Moomba Festival in Melbourne. She had become a nurse and was married, with two children.)

We knew it was impossible to return to the east to protect our sideshow space. But the Western Australian Showman's Guild, which had been formed a few years earlier, offered to fund us with rent-free show space to help get us back on our feet. This was certainly more than the Showman's Guild of Australia had offered us by way of help.

Looking over what vehicles we had left, we found that the little bus had all but given up the ghost. The engine was stuffed from all the road dust it had swallowed. The ute had gone the same way. Shopping around, we had just enough cash to buy a used 1948 3-tonne Austin truck. Finally, after repairing what gear we had managed to save, we could get back on the road – but with no caravan, car or money.

Mick spoke to me about him taking a job and looking after the kids. That way, he could keep the home fires burning while I was away with the dancing girls working the larger shows in Western Australia with our burlesque act. I was feeling stronger now, and we figured I was up to it. We wouldn't be apart for any extended period and what I earned could be put aside for a caravan and the trip back east. The other factors were that the kids needed schooling, and we couldn't pack everyone into the one truck to travel. As we weren't going to work the smaller shows in Western Australia, the girls and I would only be away for short periods, mostly weekends, and be home between shows.

With our new plan in place, Mick started work at a late-night job he had found at a nearby transport delivery company. I do believe that I had the best husband in the world. He was always thinking of us, his never-say-die family.

For our first burlesque show, the two girls and I headed for

Albany, right down on the southern coast where the whaling stations still operated.

When we arrived in Albany, a nasty wind was blowing, known as a 'Southerly Buster'. It was whipping snappy hard gusts all over the showgrounds. As the girls and I laid out the tent and waited for these gusty sea winds to subside, different show people kept giving us advice. While none of these big strong men offered to help, they were amazed to see two very cute young girls swinging sledgehammers with expertise. Instead of lifting, the girls were rolling the very heavy canvas sections into place, prior to lacing them together. They were competing very well with the fellows opposite on the boxing tent. These men kept ragging at the girls to grow muscles, so they could lift the sections instead of rolling them. But as the men went to hoist their canvas, with their boss George Stewart yelling advice, the wind hit again … and away went the boxing tent!

Realising that there was no way we could stand our tent in these wind gusts, I called the girls over to explain an idea that was used under similar circumstances by some of the old-time circus families. Then I jumped into the truck and drove down to the jetty where, after telling the fishermen of my problem and offering some free tickets to the burlesque show, they lent me a stack of heavy rope.

By the time I got back to the showgrounds, the girls had everything ready and had mated up with a group of tough young fishermen from the whaling boats. With our truck parked as a wind buffer, Colleen then put one of her new friends to work, tying off the guy ropes right along the side of the truck as extra security against the gusts. At the same time, Sandy and I got to work with the heavy ropes to secure the two king poles now protruding out of the top of the tent. By this time, we had a pretty big audience of show people watching on. Working quickly, we soon had the sidewall acting as a buffer. From there, we started securing the king poles using the borrowed rope. The showmen all rushed in to help as they now understood this unusual idea. In just a few minutes we had stood the outer side poles and tightened the tent against further strong winds. Then up went the banner poles on the outside, with the pictorials showing what our variety show is all about. After that, we collapsed in a heap. Hmm, wasn't I meant to be taking it easy?

The next morning, George Stewart called over to tell me that his boxing tent couldn't be repaired in time to work the show. It had been torn when the wind took it. He then put a proposition to me: 'What about if I run the boxing in your tent in between your burlesque shows?' He also assured me that I wouldn't be out of pocket as he would cover my rent.

'Great idea!' I said. 'One of my girls will handle the ticket box and we can split your takings.' I then informed him that, although my rent was free (the gift from the Western Australia Guild), he could still pay the 'free rent' from his share.

When we got home after that show run in late November, and I upended the takings bag, Mick couldn't believe what I had achieved. That was without a doubt one of the best country shows we had ever worked.

Chapter 20

A New Way

Early 1970s

More changes were afoot. After more than seven years with us, our gorgeous dancers Sandy and Colleen decided to head home. Mick and I knew we would miss them badly; the kids would too. But it was time. (Over the years we would hear from these wonderful women. Colleen married and settled in the town of Babinda, in the rainforest area south of Cairns. We see Sandy periodically in Abbotsford, Melbourne, where she is married with children.)

With that, we were out of business. If we were to bounce back, we had to at least hold our sideshow ground space or it would be reallocated to other showmen. With no assistance from the Showman's Guild – even though my father had helped form the organisation and Mick and I were both fully paid-up members – we sought help elsewhere. Mick contacted fellow showie John Castles (whose wife, Sis Bourke the accordionist, was a relative on Goldie's side of the family). We transferred all our space from the back country of Queensland right through to Darwin into John's name, with the private understanding that he would look after any family member of ours if the need arose, with enough space to set up on. (John is now no longer with us, but to this day his son 'Little John' honours that handshake agreement.)

Our other space, the lower run in and around Brisbane and throughout the New South Wales show runs, just disappeared! Our many years of sheer hard work had gone down the drain because an organisation that was sworn to help its own in times of need had decreed that we were not worth any assistance – because we weren't dead!

Crushed but not defeated, we focussed on family. We parked our show stuff. The ancient Austin truck and the stage trailer (now fully repaired), along with the show tents and banners, were put away in the backyard of the house we had rented in Leederville. This would be enough to work the South Australia and Victorian show runs, where we had managed to retain some of our space.

With the kids settled into school, Mick took on a much better paying job with the main roads department, driving a dump truck. So, we didn't have to touch the money we had from the Perth show and the Western Australia show run leading up to Christmas.

Then, a surprise just round the corner. Mick ran into a bloke by the name of Max McIntire. He was living with Goldie, only a suburb away from us, with both of Mick's sons also close by. Both 'boys' were now young married men, with children of their own.

Yep, Mick was a grandad. His son Michael had five little boys, while his other son Fred had a little boy, with a baby girl on the way. It was a very happy reunion.

Adding to it all, Max McIntire just happened to be my little friend who had tried to set fire to the 'Rex' building at St Mary's Convent all those years ago. To think he'd end up marrying my husband's ex and becoming my 'husband in-law'! Mind you, show people are a pretty tightknit mob – we all ended up connected somehow. Max had become known as Maxie the Lair, a cheeky bugger always dressed in a smart suit, finished off with a snappy fedora hat.

With Goldie and Max living so close, we decided we should all spend Christmas together. After weeks of pressie shopping, we turned up to their place and Mick took a back seat to allow Max to be Father Christmas, handing out all the presents. I have never seen a happier Santa.

With Goldie's two teenage girls, Sandra and Maria, plus Michael and Fred's six little kids, the excitement was high. Added to that mix were our five kids. The sounds of laugher were accompanied by the ripping of boxes and the crinkling of wrapping paper. There were gifts everywhere.

Then the pressie from me to Mick was opened. Out of the packaging came an electric Sunbeam frying pan. After much laughter, I had to open my gift from Mick. Lo and behold: an electric circular saw.

Us two crazy people got exactly what we needed. Now I could

start to rebuild our caravan, after Mick cooked me a lovely breakfast with his new frying pan. What a great day, although at one stage Goldie laughed so much, she had an asthma attack!

After this wonderful Christmas, we settled into the life of being locals. Just regular locals. But really, who were we kidding? We were showies, after all, not dump truck drivers. It was only a month or so later that Mick's son, Michael, told him about a chap who was looking for a partner to invest in a nightclub that had been closed for some time. David Goode had a long-term lease but no funds to refurbish it. Would we be interested in a partnership?

David was a fully qualified chef who had been involved in the nightclub business for many years while his wife Hazel, a professional hostess, knew just how to handle even the most boisterous patron. From our first meeting, we became firm friends and business partners.

Obviously, nothing could be done without money, so off I trotted to our bank. The upshot was that with the bank's backing, we could go ahead with the nightclub. It was now into the 1970s, and we were about to set out on an entirely new show business undertaking. One we had never tried before.

For months, Mick and David spent every hour of their free time stripping out all the old equipment and furniture, ready for a complete repainting and refurbishment. This would entail a new kitchen, bar, toilets, carpets and floor-to-ceiling drapes of a very rich, deep red brocade. Then came hidden lighting, air conditioning, and a complete revamping of the dance floor and stage, with café-style booths along one wall and upholstered chairs and dining tables surrounding the dance floor.

With David and Hazel's help, we got to know other club owners. This was a fraternity not dissimilar to the show life. We were confident we could pull together a great nightclub.

Now with money still tight, and needing even more for our upcoming grand opening, we returned temporarily to what we knew best. We organised a burlesque tent for the Perth Royal Show. It was our comeback, of sorts. Fortunately, we still had all the costumes and equipment we needed. I then recruited several dancers to back up the main artist. These girls could perform as the lovely hula-hula Tahitian dancers, 'direct from the South Sea Islands', and as the go-go girls who would shake, rattle and roll in their acrobatic contortionist-styled dancing. The star attraction would still be the striptease artist.

The stage, banners, ticket box and line-up platform were all in place. The only problem was we still didn't have a main artist. None of the strippers from the clubs were prepared to work both day and night for the long show period of seven days and nights. Such long hours required a fair amount of stamina. Time was running out. Two days before the show was to begin, Hazel contacted me. She had a girl who was prepared to work the hours. Her name was Rose Chan. She was a professional stripper from Malaysia who apparently needed a large sum of money, fast.

On meeting Rose, my first thought was that she was too old, and a bit heavy in the hips. Aged around the 40-year mark, with a well-endowed figure, I feared she would never stand up to the rigours of working a capital show. But after watching her use that body, I realised I had someone who knew how to thrill an audience. Rose proved to be a professional in every sense of the word. She worked as hard on the outside of the tent, wriggling, blowing kisses and coaxing the customers to enter, as she did on the inside, with her fascinatingly exotic dancing.

We were on a winner at the Royal Perth Show. It felt good to be back in business.

By this time, Mick had given up his roadworks job. He was working night and day with David, making final preparations for the grand opening of our nightclub: Lindy's. A simple name to remember.

The club was upstairs, on the corner of James and Fitzgerald streets in North Perth, just over what was then known as Horseshoe Bridge.

Opening night was one to remember. Our beautifully refurbished club attracted a huge and glamorous crowd. Every wall was covered in the rich red brocaded drapes cascading from floor to ceiling, with the mahogany dance floor gleaming softly under the hidden lighting.

The bandstand, although tiny, featured a beautiful baby grand piano. The opening was held on Friday, 2 October 1970. Guests included Alan Bond, who had amassed a fortune as a property developer. He would entertain prospective buyers in his nearby club, The Red Garter. Alan arrived at Lindy's with his club manager,

Freddy Mason, along with many other well-known club owners and identities like Roberta 'Bobby' Nugent, a nightclub singer and strongwoman. Other key people were our band leader David Whey and his musicians, called the Highway Ones.

Our bar manager, Rickie Smith, made sure the patrons' glasses were always full. Rickie was a wonderful operator. Whenever he poured a drink for me it was always my special, which consisted of a Bloody Mary, without the Mary, or a gin and tonic, without the gin. Then there was Joe Fenessie, our doorman and chief 'chucker-outer'. Joe was a champion wrestler in his day, with a heart of gold and the appearance of a savage pit-bull terrier. God help anyone who stepped out of line.

We had decided not to have a floor show at Lindy's, as there were other much larger clubs doing this. Rather, we felt that our club would be better off as a musicians' club, where the visiting 'musos' could have a few drinks with their friends and a meal without being harassed by other patrons. But as it happened, none of the musos could resist the urge to show off, so we had many a jam session featuring some of the top bands and singers. This was the era when pub bands were all the go. In the early 70s, hotel licences ran from 10am to 10pm Monday to Saturday, with no trading on Sundays. So, there were many musos still hyped up and needing an outlet to let off steam late at night.

Lindy's soon became the place to meet. We were packed out every night, with the bar and kitchen doing a roaring trade. At the time, there was no need for a liquor licence. Everything was very laid back. We could open at any time, usually from Tuesday until Saturday, 10pm to 6am, after the pubs were shut.

Mick and I generally headed home at about 7am, arriving just in time for all the kids to kiss and cuddle us good morning, have a good breakfast then head off to school. On their arrival home, we would be just rising from our bed after a good day's sleep.

The nights were long, but our bills were all paid and in no time the club was running smoothly. Mick was in his element, meeting and greeting the patrons as club host, along with David as our chef/host. David Whey and the Highway Ones kept the tunes going, and Hazel kept the bar staff and hostesses on their toes. My job was to act as relief chef and keep the books in order.

With our children settled down and getting an education, life was easier in many ways than the show runs. I had a fantastic, permanent live-in housekeeper/nanny, and for the first time in years I was able to relax and spend some time with my kids. But there were more good things to come.

Chapter 21

About Time!

Early 1970s

In 1971, with Lindy's going strong, a solicitor contacted us with good news. He had a date for Mick's divorce to be heard. At last! We had waited so long for this, but it was only possible because of free legal help finally offered by the War Service Department.

The big day finally arrived, to a packed courtroom. There were several divorce cases to be heard, and we were about halfway down the agenda. At the lunch break, our solicitor said, 'Things aren't looking too good. No divorces have been granted today.' Looking at me, he asked, 'How do you feel about being called?'

I answered with a shrug. 'Okay. What sort of a problem could it be to answer a few questions truthfully?'

Eventually it was our time. Our solicitor spoke at length to the bewigged judge regarding what had led to Mick's break-up with Goldie. He then spoke eloquently about our life together and our desire to legally become man and wife.

Then he called for me to take the stand. I took the oath and the judge started asking his questions. 'When did you first meet Mr Brophy?' 'Did you ever get to meet his wife?' 'How do you feel about his older children?'

Then the cruncher. The judge, looking directly at me, asked 'During the past fifteen years, to the best of your knowledge, did Mr Brophy ever have marital relations with Mrs Goldie Brophy?'

Instantly I was on my feet, a red haze flashing before my eyes. I slammed my fist down and yelled at the top of my voice, 'He'd better bloody well not have!'

I don't remember leaving the court room.

'What happened?' I asked, sitting outside in a daze.

'I'll tell you what happened, Norma,' said our lawyer. 'After your outburst, the judge didn't hesitate. Divorce granted! He was barely able to contain his grin, and the public were clapping! Well done, Norma!'

Three months later, Mick and I were married. We had a beautiful ceremony in the tiny timbered Methodist church in Subiaco, which Mick had attended as a child.

I was dressed in a finely woven wool suit of cream slacks and a knee-length sleeveless 'vest style' jacket, with cream leather high-heels and an adorable long-sleeved pure silk blouse in the softest shade of pink. (As I had been engaged to Mick for fifteen years, and during that time had produced five beautiful children, I felt that a long, white virginal wedding dress would not have been appropriate.) I was so fortunate that some of my nightclub friends were qualified hairdressers. My platinum blonde hair was tinted with just a hint of pink and swept up into a very modern beehive bouffant style. I carried a single pink rose to complete my ensemble.

My matron of honour, Hazel Goode, was also dressed in a two-piece cerise slacks suit. Mick wore a three-piece pinstripe suit of deep blue, looking the very elegant and smart nightclub proprietor that he was.

Hazel and I travelled to the church in a London taxi (better known in England as a 'hackney coach'). It was owned and driven by my mate, the strongwoman 'Bobby' Nugent, dressed in a full English-style chauffeur's uniform.

I was walked down the aisle by Mick's brother, Jim, who I think was the proudest man in the church. Dressed in lovely new outfits, our five children sat beaming in the front row, attended to by their aunts and uncles.

The celebrations began at the Leederville Hotel, with all nibbles supplied by this well-known working man's pub. By 7pm, we moved on to The Red Garter nightclub, along with a huge gathering of show people and nightclub friends, plus a large number of 'do-drop-ins'. It seemed no one was going to miss being part of our wedding.

The reception at the Red Garter, with all liquor supplied, was our wedding gift from Alan Bond, my husband's drinking partner. Another great gift came from the prestigious Savoy Hotel in Hay Street, where we had two nights' accommodation. This was the hotel where Mick's dad had worked as head barman for over twenty years. (A further special present awaited us at the hotel. It came from David, Hazel, and a large group of car dealers and pub owners – all long-time friends of David's – who had the room filled with bouquets of beautiful flowers. The satin sheets on the bed were covered with them. The perfume was exquisite.)

Using the Red Garter's kitchen, David put on a most elaborate wedding feast, after which the kids were returned home to sleep, with their nanny to care for them. The celebrations then ran right through until the evening of the next day.

David was also the MC at the reception, and doing a wonderful job announcing the various gifts, when he finally opened a large envelope. Going silent for a few moments, he absorbed the contents. Inside the envelope was a long-term lease for a business directly opposite the Red Garter nightclub. Also enclosed was a hand-written note from local madam Shirley Finn, stating that the place was fully functional and open for business.

A former butcher shop, this building had been empty for many years until Shirley had acquired it to sell a different type of goods. (Wink wink.) So, it was quite natural for her many customers to still refer to it as 'the Butcher Shop'.

The staff of the Butcher Shop had already been notified as to who the new property managers were. They couldn't be happier and gathered around both Mick and I, assuring us that they would continue to work hard – and not just lie on their backs.

Even after the initial shock, followed by the ribald comments, shouting and laughter, it took Mick and I some time before we could get anywhere near Shirley to decline her rather magnificent offer. Neither Mick nor I could ever see ourselves in the role of brothel keepers. Even for us, it would have been more trouble than it was worth!

We found out later that two detectives had slipped in to our reception. Brothels weren't their business, however. They were tailing one of our old showie guests. Wally had travelled interstate by train to come to our wedding. On arrival at Perth station, he was met by the detectives. You see, Wally was wanted on a few charges. Well, he wasn't going to miss the Brophy wedding, so he struck a deal with the coppers.

'Come on, fellas,' he'd said. 'You can't nab me now. I'm going to Mick and Norma's wedding! Look, here's my suit.'

'Mick and Norma who?'

'Mick and Norma Brophy of Lindy's!'

The detectives went from looking stern to looking outright offended. 'What the hell? Why weren't we invited? We're regulars at that club. We're coming with you! You can go to the wedding and reception, but you have to promise not to take off.'

Wally gave them his word and stuck to it. Although rumour had it that after the reception, he still managed to duck across to the Butcher Shop for a 'constitutional'.

Now husband and wife, with the piece of paper to prove it, Mick and I were in seventh heaven. We finally had our finances under control. The club was paying for itself. Life was good.

Then came a kick in the guts: liquor licensing of all nightclubs in Western Australia and the extension of late-night hours for hotels. The pubs could now stay open until midnight, with all clubs having to shut on the dot of 2am. Just when Lindy's was starting to warm up!

As if this wasn't bad enough for the nightclub scene, at the end of 1972, football clubs were granted liquor licences as well. Well, no guessing, Christmas fell flat for us that year. The new rules were in play and we had to abide by them or suffer the hefty fines. It was a cruel blow for the small clubs.

We secured a liquor licence, and Lindy's struggled on, but the heady days and nights were over. We couldn't make enough from the club to survive on our share. We talked it over with David and Hazel, who decided to tough it out as they knew no other life. A buyer was found for our half of the business. (There's always someone willing to buy into a lost cause thinking they can change it.) It was a little over two years since the place had opened, and now we were done.

Within twelve months, many clubs had closed their doors. Unfortunately, Lindy's was one of them. We got out at the right time.

A tragic side story played out four years after our wedding. In 1975, Shirley Finn was found dead in her car on a Perth golf course. She'd been killed gangland-style, with four bullets to the back of the head. She was only thirty-three. She had been threatening to blow the whistle on illegal dealings by police, businessmen and politicians. After a royal commission, several cold-case reviews and an inquest, the coroner found in 2020 that there were 'too many suspects'. The case remains unsolved. Fact is often stranger than fiction. RIP Shirley Finn.

Chapter 22

Rebuilding Our Lives

Early–mid 1970s

With our nightclub dreams dashed, it was time to put our thinking caps back on. We wanted to move out of the city and settle the kids in some good schools. Shayne and Kym were now both high school students. The three boys were all in primary school. We wanted something where we were all together and not having to split the family up so often. What could we do? Then it came to us.

After weeks of searching, we found what we were looking for. It was a café on the edge of Brunswick Junction, a tiny town on a busy road between the larger towns of Harvey and Bunbury, a couple of hours from Perth. It was ideally set up to be turned into a truck stop, which we named Mick's Dine-O-Mat.

Leading off the kitchen was a family lounge, three bedrooms, bathroom, laundry and carport, with a big storage shed in a large backyard. There was a primary school within a few blocks and a bus service to the high school in nearby Harvey.

Within a few weeks we had signed a two-year lease and moved in. The kids loved it; once again they had their dad and mum with them full time.

For the next year and a half, it was no effort at all to get the older kids to serve in the café after school. They would sit at one of the tables in the dining area to do their homework and would even have their new friends over to help them serve when needed.

In Brunswick Junction, our family were regarded as eccentrics. And no doubt the town was probably right. But our kids, over the short few years we were there, managed to get a reasonable amount of education.

Shayne at fifteen was one of only five students in all of Western Australia to be awarded a highly sought-after high school academic award. Even now after so many years, I feel great pride in her achievement.

Overall, life was so much more relaxing. We got back to being a real family again. Mick and I both accepted that we would never become millionaires in the café, but we were happy enough. Or so I thought.

Even though Mick hadn't been born a showman, he couldn't get the wanderlust out of his system. Sure enough, he wandered into the kitchen one day with another one of his ideas. 'How much money do we have in the kitty, love?' he asked.

After a lot of fumbling and mumbling, he finally came out with it. 'There are lots of markets and weekend sales being held all around

Bunbury,' he explained. 'We could buy some mini-motorbikes and run them as a ride at these events. What do you think?'

Before I could answer, in came the clincher. 'It'd give our boys something to do. They're old enough now, so they could help me run the bikes on the weekends.'

Before I knew it, Mick had the old Austin truck out of hibernation and loaded up with six brand new minibikes. Having obtained permission from the Bunbury markets for a small fee, he was ready to roll with his new little show ride.

Over the next year, our boys, and quite often Kym, worked the bikes while Mick, the proud father, sat back in the ticket box. Shayne and I were left to work the café. But Mick was right again; the bikes proved to be a winner.

Slowly but surely, we were revving up for a return to the showie life. We opted not to renew the lease on the café. It was obvious that not only Mick but also the kids were mad keen to get back on the road again.

Renting a house in Swanbourne, just down the road from the Perth showgrounds, we arranged with the show society to occupy an old shed, where Mick could store a Ford truck he had bought to replace the old Austin. The plan was to convert it into a camper van. The shed also had plenty of room to store the minibikes when the boys weren't playing around on them, under the guise of testing them out.

After settling in, the kids again enrolled in the nearby school. We knew that once back on the road we would again be dependent on the correspondence system, which was hit and miss at the best of times.

After booking some space for both the minibikes and the snake show at the upcoming Perth Royal Show, we revamped the snake tent and its pictorial banners. A fair bit of spit and polish was needed. And I had to go snake hunting again. Once again, I could do what I did best, that is, run a sideshow tent – even if it was in a pit full of slithering reptiles.

The kids worked their little bums off preparing for the annual show. Our fourteen-year-old tomboy Kym was placed in charge of the minibikes, with her three younger brothers to assist. Meantime, Shayne was begging us to allow her to work in the snake pit. As a young girl, she had proven herself to be an extremely competent reptile handler when helping me search for snakes and lizards. We finally relented, but on the understanding that I would always be in the pit with her. And only after she had studied up on Australian snakes and their venom.

The Snake Tent show went extremely well at the 1974 Perth Show. Shayne was a sensation, drawing huge crowds each day of the show. The fact she was only sixteen drew lots of attention and generated great publicity. Over at the minibikes ride, the other kids were in complete control, while their dad boasted about his four little mechanics.

With the Ford truck refurbished, we soon had a campervan with enough room for all our children, and a shower. Plus, it could tow a caravan, which Mick had picked up cheap. Completing our convoy, we still had the trailer, towed by the station wagon, to carry our show gear.

Where we would go, and what we were going to do when we got there, we had no idea. We just knew that with the earnings from the show and our savings, it was time the Brophys were proper showies again.

Luck was with us. An old friend, Glen Salter, had just arrived in Perth. Mick had first met Glen when he did some mechanical work on one of our trucks in Goondiwindi years before. Noting his excellent repairs, Mick had introduced Glen to some showmen. Glen then stayed on the show circuit as a travelling mechanic, repairing many of the show people's vehicles, and he was now working as the permanent mechanic for Circus Royale.

The big circus had just arrived in Western Australia for the Easter school holidays. Well, the long and the short of it was that Mick went with Glen to the circus lot to meet the owner, Frank Gasser. The first thing Mick noticed was that they had no carnival at the front of the tent. Racing home, he made the announcement: 'We're going to join the circus.'

The first place we showed in with Circus Royale was in the suburb of Midland. Mick very quickly put together a couple of games. So, along with the snake tent show and the minibikes, we had a small but reasonable carnival to dress up the front of the circus.

Over the many months we travelled with Frank Gasser and his family, he refused any rental from the carnival, although we did reimburse him in other ways, like some signwriting.

The Gassers had only recently opened their circus. Along with Frank's brothers, Anton and Sonny and their families, they had headed across the Nullarbor to find fresh ground away from the circuses working throughout the eastern states. The entire Gasser family were all true international performers who had put together a wonderful, well-organised circus, complete with other international artists.

Frank and his wife Manuela were both performers who began their craft in a family circus in Switzerland. They came to Australia in the mid-1960s, performing with Bullen's Circus. By 1974, Frank's brother Anton had joined them for a new act known as 'the Swiss Aerialists', which was a centre-arena attraction at the Royal Melbourne Show.

Within a few years, Frank and Manuela had their own show on the road, naming it Circus Royale after their circus back in Switzerland. (In 1980, Frank invited another circus family, the Bellis, to come and work with him in Australia. The Belli clan – Rudi Belli, a circus animal trainer, and his four daughters and wife, Mona, who made up a truly amazing troupe known as the Kan-Tei sisters – arrived in time for Frank to be naturalised as an Australian citizen. A ceremony was held in his circus tent in front of a huge audience in Penrith, presided over by the mayor.)

It didn't take long for our kids to mix in at the circus, with Warren forever juggling something. At training sessions, mostly held after each evening performance, the kids had the time of their lives learning the art of performing before an audience. The sessions were generally attended by Manuela's eldest boy, Carlos, along with trainee trapeze artists Sonja and Heidi, the children of performers Ron and Pearl Gluck. Manuela Gasser was a stickler for timing, with Frank an outstanding balancing artist, determined to pass on his knowledge to the kids. Our little Ashley was right up for it. He'd been eyeing off the high-wire since he was seven years old. No fence was safe with Ashley around. Even barbed wire held no fear for him.

One day, when Ashley was around seven years old, Mick and I were driving up to the campsite after shopping and saw him walking along a barbed-wire fence! I quietly came up behind him, and as soon as he safely reached a fence post, I said firmly, 'What the hell do you think you're doing? Get down from there!'

'But Mum, I'm wire walking, and I'm good! I want to be a tightwire walker when I grow up.'

After I walked back to Mick, I said, 'Well, if he wants to wire walk, let's get him doing it the hard way.'

From then on, every time we pulled up in camp, we parked our two trucks tail to tail and strung a wire tightly from tow ball to tow ball, a foot off the ground. Ashley practised on that wire non-stop. Sure, he fell off a lot – that's why it was only one foot high! Eventually he was doing back somersaults. His path was set to follow his dream to become a tightwire walker.

While Kym had less interest in the circus – she spent her time helping her dad with the carnival gear – Shayne loved the trapeze bars and, of course, her snakes. She also became the tutor for all the primary school kids in the circus. Since Shayne was already helping her brothers with correspondence lessons, Manuela asked if she might take on a few more kids. Of course, she would. This was to be Shayne's first paid job.

A spare caravan was set up as a little classroom, with seats, desks and the mandatory blackboard. The kids arrived early for their first day, full of excitement. They had their very own circus school. Shayne had ushered them in and started the lesson when there was a violent hammering at the door. Four-year-old Sandro Gasser was in a temper. He had been locked out! Well, he wasn't going to cop that. With a mighty 'thunk', the caravan started rolling backwards down the sloping ground. Little Sandro had pulled the chocks from behind the caravan wheels and released the brake. He'd shown them. They weren't going to have fun in the school room without him!

Shayne soon had her classroom back in order, but it was a different story in the snake pit. During one of our shows, she attempted my old trick of looping a snake into a knot. But she was doing it with a tiger snake, one of the most venomous snakes in Australia! Well, that was the end of that. No more snake shows for our Shayne.

The snakes weren't the only animals to watch out for. One day, while we were set up at Midland Junction on the outskirts of Perth, the circus elephant, Tanya, decided it was time to take off. In the early hours of the morning, while everyone slept, Tanya went for a stroll right down the middle of the great Northern Highway, heading for the city. With the morning traffic all around her, Tanya was starting to get excited. She began to trumpet, stamp and sway all over the road as the traffic backed up in all directions.

The local policeman was in a bit of a panic, so he radioed his base, yelling into the handset: 'There's a huge elephant loose on the Great Northern and it's heading for Perth!'

Base very calmly answered back, 'Is it a pink elephant?'

The Show Schools

Until the year 2000, travelling show people had great difficulty educating their children through the Primary Correspondence School system. They could not connect with the School of the Air as they did not have the facilities. So, they had to rely entirely on the postal service, and the school returning their children's work on time in whichever town they had nominated.

Eventually a group of travelling show women (including, among others, Julie Cheyne, Narelle Hennessy, Ruth Johnson, Leanne Allen, Glynis Jackson, Kym Silver and Narelle March) began a campaign to improve the situation. These women were determined that all show children would have the education that many before them had been denied.

Throughout the 1990s, and after endless meetings with state and federal education department officials, the women lobbied and eventually won. The result was that in January 2000, two mobile schools with fully equipped transportable classrooms joined the show circuits, complete with a principal, teachers and a driver/maintenance man.

Affiliated with distance education schools and the School of the Air, the Queensland School for Travelling Show Children (QSTSC) would provide education for children on show circuits in all states and territories of Australia except Western Australia.

For twelve years, these schoolrooms operated under the leadership of a wonderful headmistress, Cathy Fullerton. The children bloomed as they never had before and very proudly wore their uniforms to their own school each day.

Both of the trailerised schools came with satellite dishes to relay all the information back to distance education hubs, where the students' work could be assessed as it came to hand. The show children were finally getting the recognition that all Australian school children were entitled to.

Then, in 2012, the show people saw their children's world come crashing down. After twelve years of exemplary teaching, the School for Travelling Show Children was closed. This came as a complete shock; the classrooms, complete with two prime mover vehicles, and all their state-of-the-art equipment were taken and stored in a large open paddock on the outskirts of Brisbane, where they remained exposed to extreme weather conditions.

Despite an outcry from showfolk, the plight of the children was ignored by those responsible in the Queensland government. In the show people's eyes, the powers that be had shut the mobile schools down without any valid logic. The only reasoning seemed to be that the schools were too expensive to run.

After two years exploring every avenue possible, the issue became a federal matter as the ladies on the committee had their concerns heard by the education department in Canberra.

Finally, the show people had their classrooms back on the road again, after expensive refitting. The schools are now registered as private with the Federal Government and function under the name of the National School for Travelling Show Children (NSTSC). These are the only travelling schools of their kind in the world that educate large numbers of show children from prep through to grade six.

Chapter 23

The Circus Goes On

Mid 1970s

Eventually the time came for us to leave the Gassers. They were heading back east and it wasn't viable for us to take on that awfully long trip. So, we linked up with another circus, Perry Bros, which was heading north for the mining towns.

The Perrys had established their circus in the 1800s and were known as one of the oldest traditional circuses to have performed non-stop in Australia, even throughout two world wars.

Their family and ours became close friends, with our kids practising brand new acts so as to become part of the Perry Bros 'family'. (Our son Warren eventually married Yasmin Perry-Maynard and produced three exceptionally talented sons. They now run their own circus, Brophy Bros Circus.)

Jim and Nell Perry and their family were from the old school of animal trainers, with a herd of three elephants, performing lions, dogs and ponies. All of these were cared for by seventy-year-old Jim and his son-in-law Fred Maynard (who was married to Jim and Nell's daughter, Lorraine).

On the road north with the Perrys, we were heading for the mining town of Port Newman when suddenly our windscreen was filled with fluttering paper. Mick immediately pulled up and we found to our amazement that this paper was banknotes of various denominations, one dollar up to twenty dollars, scattered all along the road.

Hardly believing our eyes, we rushed to gather as many bills as we could, stuffing them into our shirts. Then it hit us. There had been no other traffic on this very quiet road, so the money could only have come from Nell Perry's caravan, which was travelling ahead of us.

Mick sprang into action. 'You stay here, my pet, and keep grabbing that money on the road. I'll catch old Nell and stop her.' With that, he jumped into the truck and took off. Here I was alone, on a deserted back country bush track, with no food or water. More than an hour later, he returned with Nell and we got the whole story. Her truck had hit a ditch and lurched sideways, slamming the caravan into a boulder on the side of the road. After inspection, the damage appeared minimal, so Nell kept driving. Little did she know there was now a gaping hole in the floor of the caravan. Beside that hole, the takings box for the entire show run had upended, with all the money being sucked out as she drove.

After some makeshift repairs, and a thorough search of the

entire area, this grand old lady of the circus thanked us all by yelling at the top of her voice, 'Come on everyone, playtime is over! Now it's time to hit the road!'

She was certainly a tough old girl, and she is now buried in the cemetery of Greta, Victoria, the hometown of the infamous bushranger Ned Kelly. Being only a few graves apart, I am sure they often swap tales about the good old days.

After showing throughout the top end of Western Australia with Perrys, we linked up with Lennon's Circus, which was bound for the eastern states after doing the Perth Royal Show. This suited us fine as the Perth show would give us the finances we needed for the long trip from one side of Australia to the other.

Over the months that followed, Shayne mastered the art of performing on a trapeze bar, high above the circus arena, and became part of the Lennon show. At the same time, she had her eye on a handsome young bloke, Wayne Halliday, the stepson of the circus owner himself, Lindsey Lennon.

By the time we arrived in the eastern states, Shayne and Wayne were engaged.

Having made it all the way to outback Queensland with Lennon's Circus, we weren't too eager to continue on to Darwin as the distances were huge. Shayne, however, had other ideas. She was staying on with the circus – the first of our brood to fly the nest. I knew she was in good hands, and Wayne definitely wouldn't let her tie a tiger snake into a knot!

Mick and I, with the three boys and Kym, farewelled Lennon's

Circus in March 1976, bound for the small town of Gatton, south-east of Brisbane. There we spent three months making costumes, building props and bringing together all the fundamentals for the next phase in our lives. We were about to re-invent ourselves again.

Chapter 24

Climbing the Ladder

Mid–late 1970s

After all our time amidst the various circus families, we were now out on our own. With the Brophy kids as the stars of their own show, we became Brophy Bros Circus Attractions.

Our first performance was at the 1977 Pacific Fair carnival in Townsville, which was run by an old showie mate, Noel McGregor. The crowd gathered close around our small open-air arena to watch as our four children entertained them in a half-hour show. Ashley opened the show with his daring Roller Boller Balancing Act, doing handstands and somersaults on a skateboard, six feet above the ground on a small platform. Next were the lovable clowns, Mr McGazza and his sister Kymbo (Gary and Kym), in their tremendously funny Telescopic Water Gag, which ended up with the audience being sprayed with water. This was followed by Wazza (Warren) juggling while pedalling his seven-foot-high unicycle, which he'd made himself with a helping hand from his dad. Gary returned for the finale, as the Rhinestone Cowboy, with his fancy rope-spinning. His whip-cracking provided a noisy and exciting finish to the show.

The show was a resounding success. From this, our very first attempt at being professional circus performers, we continued along what was known as the Safari Run in Queensland. As crowd pullers for Noel's carnival, we worked forty-eight half-hour free circus performances at the next ten towns. And what a drawcard to the carnivals we were.

From this promising start, it was now my job to approach more venues, to sell them the idea of having our circus as free entertainment for their show-going public. Our acts weren't big enough for the main arena at the agricultural shows but, as I pointed out to the venue owners, we could perform ringside, allowing the public to get up close and personal with the circus folk.

These huge show arenas were the domain of stuntmen such as Darky Harrison, the father of a troupe of young stuntmen and women who would defy death in the most incredible feats of acrobatic gymnastics. They were like monkeys, racing up a 60-foot smooth steel pole without any safety nets or harnesses, then going into a series of handstands.

Another main arena attraction was the giant truck named the Waltzing Matilda, fitted with a Rolls Royce jet engine. Its owner and driver Ray Kernaghan raced it around at incredible speeds of more than 300 kilometres per hour. Ray's son Lee became great friends with my kids, who were often passengers in the Matilda on practice runs. (Lee would go on to become one of Australia's top-ranking country singers.)

In our off times, the Beenleigh showgrounds became our home, only a short drive south of Brisbane. There the boys continually honed their acts and I made new costumes while awaiting answers to the many letters and brochures we had mailed out.

For our next show run around Brisbane, Mick approached Frank Foster of sideshow fame and came away with a circus tent on 'circus terms', that is, to pay later. I then machine stitched rolls of canvas into banners while Mick and the boys made up the banner poles and built a mobile stage to go in the tent. My next job was to paint pictorials on the banners to describe our new show. Finally, we set off with our first circus sideshow, to the small town of Monto, inland from Bundaberg.

From there, we went to the Moura Rodeo followed by the Mundubbera Show. What a kick in the backside it turned out to be. We didn't earn enough to pay the rent. After a month on the road, we had no money coming in except for Mick's Tin Can Alley game, which he worked in the sideshow area whenever possible. We had reached rock bottom before, but this was the dregs. Still, at least we could eat.

After working the last two shows at Gayndah and Biloela, it was back to Beenleigh – the showman's graveyard. We had nowhere else to go.

Struggling on into 1978, Brophy Bros Circus Attractions slowly became known as we worked some of the agricultural shows and festivals in Queensland and northern New South Wales. By this time, Ashley had also perfected his high-wire act and was known as Australia's youngest tightwire performer. We were managing to pick up some work, but it was a hard slog.

Then good ol' Mick thought of something, as usual! He asked me about an old-time circus act, 'The Revolving Ladder', which he'd heard about long ago. It hadn't been performed for many years. But it got me thinking.

With Joe Perry from Sole's Circus passing through town at the time, we sought his advice. Though Joe was really pleased with our idea, he did point out that this was an extremely dangerous act. However, he had heard a great deal about our kids performing and he was confident that they were ready. This was high praise indeed.

It turned out that Joe had a complete revolving ladder structure ready to work, packed on one of his trucks and taking up space. We were welcome to it if we felt that our kids could learn an act on it. Could they? Absolutely!

This particular act had been performed by two comedians known as Slip and Slide. They were a laugh-a-minute act, dressed as house painters in splattered overalls, complete with buckets of paint and brushes.

Our boys put together an entirely different routine. It involved Gary, under the name Mr McGazza, dressed as a down-and-out clown in a badly torn baggy suit. Warren was dressed as a voluptuous woman named Wilma, with an overabundance of lip gloss and an extremely large front to 'her' costume. They began the act with a slapstick routine, using hand signals as they chased each other around and around until they noticed a huge 20-foot ladder set up to one side. Rushing up the ladder together, and after a comedy of choreographed errors, they wound up straddling the ladder several metres apart, high above the ground. The ladder was connected by a central axle to upright posts, pegged firmly into the ground. The pair then went into a routine of high-jinx, with the ladder revolving at high speed. For the finale, Wilma jumped from one end of the ladder onto the ground, sending Mr McGazza flipping over and over and left hanging on for dear life by his legs.

(That original revolving ladder became part of one of the greatest aerial acts ever, performed by 'The Flying Angels' – a four-man high-wire motorbike aerial stunt show. More about this later.)

Just before we debuted our ladder act at the Ipswich Show, Mick came up with another idea. 'Let's rebuild the steel frame of the ladder and turn it into a self-supporting structure!' He pointed out that the ladder could then be erected without being pegged to the ground. This would make it more stable and allow the act to be performed indoors, particularly at the various shopping centres that were now opening in all the major cities.

Gary, now sixteen, had become proficient with a welder and felt confident that he was up to the task. Of course, it didn't take long for a few of the show guys to come wandering over to see what this kid was up to. One of the showmen, Keith Nocen, pointed out a few minor mistakes Gary was making. If he liked, Keith said he would show Gary how to knit the welds properly. Gary learnt so much that day, thanks to a man kind enough to take the time to teach a young show kid who was willing to learn.

After achieving this herculean task, Gary, along with his two younger brothers, built a self-supporting tightwire structure, also to be used indoors along with the ladder act.

This new set-up enabled Ashley to achieve some amazing stunts, such as performing not only the back somersault but also the near-impossible forward somersault, on a tightwire two metres above the ground. (In later years, Ashley would perform 50 metres above ground level, claiming many world records.)

It wasn't unusual for show kids to take on tasks that even adults would think twice about, especially in our family. Needless to say, we had a few accidents and some close shaves.

During a performance at the small mining town of Emerald in north-west Queensland, Warren, as Wilma the clown, miscued as he jumped off the spinning ladder. It caught him with a resounding whack. In a split second, Gary hoisted his brother onto his back, smiling and waving as Wilma was piggy-backed from the arena. There was wild applause from the audience, who had no idea that Warren had broken his leg.

Another near-disaster occurred when we headed across to the Queensland coast for a run of shows. Having finished performing at the Bowen show, we were having a quiet night sharing our campfire with friends when a young showman wandered over. We will simply call him 'Jack', out of respect for his large show family. Jack was pretty much a hothead, and had been drinking rather heavily. Earlier in the day, egged on by mates, Jack had been causing a stir at a stall being worked by Mick's adult son, Fred. Now that Jack was back to stir up more trouble, Mick stepped in, demanding he leave and sleep it off. Eventually Jack, while mouthing off threats, moved on. As ten-year-old Ashley came out of our caravan, asking me what was going on, I heard a shout from Normie Porter, one of the boxers. 'Norma, watch out!' I grabbed Ashley and threw him headfirst into the caravan as shotgun slugs ploughed through my dressing gown, missing both Ashley and me by a fraction. At that same moment, Kym and Fred fell to the ground. Jack had shot both with a double-barrelled shotgun.

In the uproar that followed, we rushed to get the wounded pair to hospital. The police were notified and he was finally apprehended in the early hours of the morning. If he had been standing any closer when he fired that gun, he would have been tried for murder, as that shotgun would have torn us all to pieces.

Fred sustained injuries from his calf to his hips, while to this day, Kym carries slugs in both of her legs. Jack was charged with 'firing a weapon in a public place'. He was given a suspended sentence. No mention was made of the fact that while Jack was being tried, his two victims were in the operating theatre of the Bowen Hospital undergoing surgical procedures.

Jack was handed a much heavier sentence from our family – he was ordered to leave the life of show business and never to return.

With poor brother Frank buried in Bowen, it was horrifying to think how close we came to burying another Brophy here.

Making our way to Newcastle, we got our first real break. The manager of the Garden City shopping centre had a special birthday event planned. Could we slot him in? Absolutely! We then followed up with a solid booking for Wyong Plaza, the next town along our way. Stopping in Sydney, we stayed with friends who suggested we check out Kings Cross. Okay, I was prepared for anything, so why not? That night, I met the fabulous drag queen Carol Byron, better known as Carlotta, and tied up a booking to perform later the following year at her nightclub, The Tender Trap.

The next day, I headed for the huge Miranda Shopping Centre. It had a massive central area with three storeys of open space, ideal for the Revolving Ladder. I met with the manager Lou Carawana, who introduced me to the boss of all Grace Bros stores, John Hancock. After a lengthy discussion on the space and height required, I was informed that they would require thirty performances, split up over six shopping centres, from late December through to late January. Could we handle that?

What a silly question. We could fly to the moon if we had to.

The past was behind us, the future looking good. We were forever the optimists.

Chapter 25

From Canberra to Kings Cross

1980

Before we knew it, we were performing non-stop at one shopping centre after the other, with a few festivals and shows thrown helter-skelter into the mix. We were now actually managing to pay the boys some wages.

Kym, now aged eighteen, announced she was in love and off to follow her heart. This beau of hers was in a show business family we had known all our lives, so he was no stranger. His name was John Foster. So Kym left us to be with John. Both our girls had flown the coop.

Then came a bigger offer, with strings attached. The 1980 Royal Canberra Show wanted us as an exclusive. The deal was that we were not to work any other venue within a radius of 200 kilometres.

Well, that was easier said than done. We were already booked for Queanbeyan, Tumut and Yass. Those three shows – all within the forbidden radius of Canberra – added up to more income than we were to receive in the capital. So, we put our thinking caps on. Surely there was a way around this.

We ended up offering Canberra the exclusive rights (for a fair consideration) to perform under canvas. We'd perform at the other three shows in the open air, as had earlier been agreed to. Canberra agreed. Bingo! What I didn't know at the time was that on opening night in the capital, we would be performing before the Prime Minister, Malcolm Fraser, and his entourage.

Our three boys performed at their supreme best in Canberra that night; they didn't miss a beat, not even when they shook hands with the PM after their final performance. (Over the following few years, our boys had the opportunity to perform before other big names in politics, including Bob Hawke, Paul Keating and John Howard. There were more, but I'd be name-dropping.)

As we headed into Easter, we heard from Carlotta's management team. Would we consider a single performance as the opening to the Fabulous Carlotta's Gaieties in Kings Cross?

Could we? Would we? Bloody hell, of course we would. Especially as we were just down the road, doing some 'freebie' gigs at the Royal Easter Show.

What Carlotta wanted was very simple really, just some freshly made fairy floss on sticks and, during the floor show, a couple of clowns to entertain her guests. The fairy floss was to be handed to guests as they entered the beautifully decorated (in circus style) cabaret nightclub, The Tender Trap. This wasn't quite our usual scene, but the price was right and the boys were keen as mustard.

The night kicked off with Carlotta making a grand, if unconventional, entrance. She stepped out of her limo, beautifully dressed and made up, juggling a huge bundle of balloons. On spying Gary, who was standing by in his clown outfit, she said, 'Oh, sweetie, can you help me with these balloons?' Gary, always the gentleman, immediately went to assist her. But Carlotta wanted the balloons hung high on the entrance wall – so high that Gary had to lift her. Placing his hands on each side of her waist, he hoisted her up when suddenly she slipped. As arms, legs and bum slid in every direction, Gary's hand accidentally gripped a vital part of Carlotta's anatomy. No harm done, but plenty of giggles. The balloons were finally secured, and Carlotta had a big smile on her face, despite the fall.

In the circus-themed foyer, Ashley greeted Carlotta and her guests with pink clouds of fairy floss. Warren delighted one and all as Wilma the clown, complete with blow-up breasts.

The cabaret opened with a bang, as Carlotta regaled the huge audience with a full description of the fun in the foyer. Then Gary and 'Wilma' were invited to give a full demonstration of how Gary managed to lift, catch and, err, handle the situation. The audience went wild for this impromptu addition to the cabaret show. It was certainly a night to remember.

Brophy Bros Attractions was the talk of the town. Our slogan became: 'Thinking entertainment? Think Brophy Bros.' We might as well have added: 'We'll try anything once.'

By now our little circus show had become an asset to the

shopping malls. We were a guaranteed drawcard, filling the big retail centres on every performance. On many occasions, it was standing room only, with even the shopkeepers and their staff keen to watch our show.

At these shopping centres, we often rubbed shoulders with consummate entertainers who were doing free shows. One of these was Jeanne Mitchell, known professionally as Jeanne Little. An award-winning entertainer and TV personality, she was a real hoot. Her catchphrase was 'Darrrrling', which perfectly matched her over-the-top fashion and bubbly personality. The funny thing was that people often got me and Jeanne mixed up. We looked alike. I am not kidding you. One time, at a shopping centre show, the two of us were standing in front of a fire escape of all places when a chap from a newspaper came up. Looking confused for a moment, he said to me, 'Lovely to meet you, Jeanne.' Well, I threw Jeanne a quick glance and she gave me a cheeky nod. So, I played along and got interviewed as Jeanne Little!

When the reporter headed off, none the wiser, Jeanne said to me, 'I should hire you, Norma. You can take over. I get sick of answering questions!'

Chapter 26

Brophy Bros Saddle Up

Early 1980s

By the early 1980s, our boys were true professionals and were itching to spread their wings even further. It came as no surprise to us when they began to talk about starting a Wild West–style circus. It seemed the Bibby cowboy blood was flowing strong.

These three young boys had been working their guts out for almost five years, crafting their art, introducing new routines, and building and rebuilding their equipment. It was rare for them to go to the movies or to mix with others their own age, except when we met up with a circus or worked the agricultural shows – which wasn't too often as we were working mostly in the major shopping centres.

Mick and I were with them all the way. We were determined to help the boys launch their cowboy circus, or go bust trying. We had a good start in that the large white canvas tent that we had used at the Canberra Show could hold almost 500 people. With colourful sidewalls and curtains, this would become a circus tent well suited to our Wild West theme.

With a little free time between shopping centre shows, we headed to the showgrounds in Liverpool, Sydney, where we had arranged to camp, while painting up the trucks and vans for our new show. Fortunately, some old mates were also camped there. Johnny Vaughn and his wife Ann were great signwriters. As they had a few weeks to spare, we soon put them to work. No one was exempt. We needed all the help we could get.

Our three boys went to work welding up frames (known in circus parlance as 'stringers' and 'jacks') for the tiered seating in the tent. Stringers were the seating boards and jacks were the steel frames to hold the boards. The boys – now aged thirteen, fifteen and eighteen – were taking on man-sized jobs and working extremely long hours to achieve their dreams.

We bought two miniature western-styled coaches for children's rides around the tent. The coaches came complete with an enormous, enclosed trailer to carry them from town to town. One was a perfect replica of the old-time Cobb & Co coach and the other a chuck wagon.

From a horse farm up near Myrtleford, Victoria, came the perfect horses to pull the wagons. These were Welsh mountain ponies, and easy to train. This whole assembly was fairly costly but would be well worth the money as the horses would be a large part of the eye-catching display on the outside of our new circus.

It became Warren's job to break in the ponies and get them

pulling the coaches. Admittedly, he had help from a wonderful horsewoman named Dell Fisher, who gave up a great deal of her time to teach Warren the fundamentals of horse handling.

For many months we were run off our feet, putting together our new show while performing at festivals in and around Sydney. Fortunately, these were mostly one-day events, so we could continue with our preparations and still earn an income.

After the Christmas run in the shopping centres, we got word from Shayne and Wayne, who were over in Western Australia. Struggling to make a living working a small carnival out the front of Circus Royale, they were keen to join our Wild West show.

Setting off from Perth with their two tiny children, they made it as far as outback New South Wales before the motor on their truck gave out. They were stranded, with very little money. Mick went to their rescue, loading up the station wagon with all the tools necessary for stripping the truck motor down. Fortunately, Wayne was a competent mechanic, so between the two men they were able to get back on the road, with Shayne and the kids enjoying the luxury of the old station wagon to continue their trip in.

With everything assembled, we announced to the world the arrival of the Brophy Bros Wild West Circus – a brand-new big-top experience offering two hours of non-stop entertainment.

By circus standards, ours was a compact outfit. It consisted of five trucks, two panel vans and the old reliable station wagon, with a caravan or trailer towed behind each vehicle. It had taken just over a year and every penny we had to put the circus together. Mick and

I were so proud of what our sons had achieved.

Saying goodbye to John and Ann Vaughn in Sydney, we headed north to the Newcastle showgrounds, where we were to camp while we gathered our crew together. Along with Shayne and Wayne and their newly repaired truck, we brought on two young tent hands. Then there was Alan Baxter, the advance agent. It was Alan's job to travel ahead of us, booking sites with the local councils and handling the advance publicity. The rest of our circus 'family' consisted of Larry Delhuntly, an ex-boxing tent proprietor, and his partner Paula Smith, a renowned country singer.

Both Larry and Paula had wonderful voices. She would bring a life-sized gorilla (played by Larry) into her rendition of *The Lion Sleeps Tonight*, changing the wording in the song from 'the lion' to 'the gorilla'. She and Larry would have patrons in stitches as the gorilla crept up under their seats or cuddled up to a pretty girl.

Our intention was to launch our new circus in Muswellbrook, west of Newcastle, then head north for the winter months, taking in all towns until we crossed the border into Queensland. Oh, what high hopes we had, and what troubles still lay before us.

The day we moved out of Newcastle, the skies opened up with a vengeance of heavy rain and freezing weather. The block we were to show on was under water. Our Wild West show was a wash-out. Muswellbrook became our first cancellation, but not our last. We were now running on a shoestring.

Finally, the rain stopped and we were able to travel on to the dryer town of Aberdeen. There, our first show was a triumph. It proved to us that our acts could wow a crowd and our circus was on the right track.

Among the many highlights was our daughter Shayne, who added lots of glamour and daring as a solo aerial trapeze artist, and our amazing tightwire walker Ashley performing backward somersaults on the wire. Then there was the daring expertise of the juggler and unicyclist, Warren, on his now 12-foot-high unicycle. The Revolving Ladder was a big winner, performed by Gary and Warren just before interval, followed later by Ashley as a trick roller bowler balancing artist, and of course the crazy clowns with their hilarious antics. Incorporated into the show also were our trick ponies and Henry, the performing piglet. He left the kids in tears of laughter, entering the arena in a baby carriage, pushed by the glamorous Shayne. Henry performed on a seesaw and a slide, with many other tricks in between. The show came to a cracking end with Gary, the Rhinestone Cowboy, performing his whip-wielding, rope and lariat spinning.

But then, with the weather slowly improving, Alan, our advance man, had to call it quits. He was an older man and his health was in decline. He had, however, booked us for Scone, Murrurundi and Quirindi. These were all one-night stands, but it gave us two weeks' work on our way up to Queensland.

With Alan gone, Mick bravely stepped in as the advance man. My fearless husband suddenly found himself having to organise the sites, permits and rental in each town, plus the publicity with local radio stations and newspapers. He also had to arrange the hiring of toilets and garbage removal. He approached all the shops with the gift of free passes for putting a poster in their windows. Then he visited the schools, where he would hand over a bundle of free passes to be given out to the children. The daylight hours were used to contact all these people, with the nights used for travelling. It was wearying work.

By the time we reached Texas, a tobacco farming town on the Queensland border, the rain had stopped, but the temperature was only just above freezing. Putting up the tent in the icy cold was agonising. But it had to be done, as we didn't have fuel money to leave town. By 7pm, we were all set up and had been fed a good meal. But where were the patrons? There was not a soul to be seen as we gazed across the showgrounds, on a little rise above the town. What the hell were we going to do? I felt gutted, my usual optimism wavering. With Mick somewhere on the road ahead of us, and out of contact, all seemed lost.

But just before 7.30pm, as we were staring into an empty tent, Gary grabbed my arm. 'Look, Mum, look!'

Below us, heading up from town, was a long line of cars. Headlights on, they were all winding up the rise towards the showgrounds. That night, we worked to a jam-packed house and extended to the following night, to another full house. We were lucky to have a free night. It turned out that this tiny town was starved for entertainment, as the nearest picture show was miles away. Punctuality aside, Mick certainly did an excellent job of drawing a crowd in that tiny town of Texas.

Our next town was Ingleburn, about 60 kilometres up the road. Mick had arrived back to let us know he had booked sites for us all the way through to Yarraman. Dodging the larger towns, as the far bigger circuses had already billed them, he had also collected a bundle of mail from the post office. In it was an unexpected letter from the Brisbane Exhibition They wanted to hire us as a free attraction for the Ekka! Wow and double wow! We were going to have a capital show under our belt. We had finally hit the big time.

I immediately spoke by phone to Mr Ces Smallcombe, the director of the Ekka, and came to a fair price for fifty half-hour performances, divided up over the ten days of the show. Our half-hour performances under our big top would be free to the show-going public.

From Yarraman, we slowed down our bookings as I had to make a complete wardrobe of extra costumes for the Ekka. We only performed in three towns each week instead of the usual five. Finally, we headed back to Brisbane, showing at the towns along the coast.

The Ekka was a huge success. We set up in a far back corner, which was usually a dead area of the showgrounds. We now had sponsors too, including American Dairy Queen Ice-cream. We certainly changed this area from a dead end into a highly active area. Every half hour performance was packed to capacity.

We not only performed with the circus, but on the day following People's Day we were asked to put on an extra stage show, to be performed on an open-air stage in the bustling picnic ground area.

This show was all country and western, with a big focus on the three boys performing with whips and ropes, alongside a number of well-known country singers. Our job was to tie the program together and do all the announcing, under the banner of the 'Brophy Bros Wild West Show'. For this extra event we were paid top dollar.

On the last day of the show, our occasionally accident-prone Ashley was late getting back for his wire-walking act. In his rush to change costume, he didn't put his protective support on underneath. Unfortunately, as he was performing a 'spin-around', somersaulting around the wire, his nether region got tangled up. He very quickly reversed back around and speedily finished his act, leaving the audience completely unaware that he was in agonising pain. One emergency operation later, the doctors were still concerned about possible permanent damage. (Thankfully, Ashley went on to become the proud father of four adorable children.)

After the Ekka, we took time out for Ashley to get back on his feet. We also needed to reassess our position regarding the circus. The public loved our Wild West circus, but we couldn't survive by showing in the small towns.

What we needed was a much larger circus tent, with more seating and more tent hands to lighten the load on our young boys. We knew the public wanted the bigger, more daring group stunt acts. It was time to scale up.

It was so sad to have to let Larry and Paula go. They were really beaut people. As for our piglet Henry, she (yes, turned out Henry was a girl) was now a very big pig. Sold to a farmer, she gave her best performances by reproducing on a regular basis. The Welsh mountain ponies were happily taken by another circus, while the two wagons went to Gary O'Neil for display at his fun park in Liverpool.

With thirteen circuses now on the road, including the Flying Fruit Fly Circus and Circus Oz, we were facing stiff competition. But we knew we had the talent and experience to take another big step.

By August of 1983, Mick had found our dream caravan for our new phase; it was the prototype of the first extendable caravans. One entire wall in the front side section was hinged at the floor and folded out, giving an amazing amount of room in the lounge and dining area.

Our next buy was a 20-foot 'Carapark' caravan, which got our young Brophy men out of the old truck camper and into much more modern accommodation. The truck camper could now become the wardrobe/dressing and sewing room, where I would make and maintain costumes.

Over the next few years, we seemed to be in a race against time, building, developing and improving what was going to be our new, improved full-scale circus. By the mid-80s, even our regular money-earner shows were feeling the heat, with some of the tented circuses giving free, short performances in shopping centres. We knew our days as a shopping centre attraction were numbered. The pressure was on for us to find some way to set ourselves apart.

Chapter 27

Record-breaking Feats

1984–1988

As usual, our next big decision came via serendipity.

In 1984, at the Shepparton show, Gary met Noel Harris. Noel held a world record for cracking the world's largest stockwhip, which was almost four metres long. From that moment on, the cowboy in our family was determined to make his own record-breaking plaited rope stockwhip. And along the way, help get the Brophy name and new circus up in lights.

At first, how Gary was going to make this monster whip wasn't entirely clear, until we met a retired policeman with a passion for whip plaiting. This fellow, Glen Denham, kindly offered to assist all three of the young Brophy men in making this monumental object.

Glen had all three boys at his home, where they set up a platform in a huge gum tree, 20 feet above the ground, with a work bench directly below. This was where all the slicing of the cowhides was to be done. A pulley was then set up to feed the lengths of leather strips up to the platform, where Gary and Glen started plaiting strands of leather around the rope belly. Down below, Warren and Ashley kept the leather strands untangled and fed more strips up as they were needed. After weeks of work, 'The Giant Australian Whip' was finished. We will be forever grateful for Glen's expertise and hard work.

With the huge whip as star attraction, we put together a special three-man performance. I spent many a night at the sewing machine, making matching three-piece suits for the boys, styled on the American gamblers' suits of the Wild West.

Arrangements were made to hold our event on the main day of the agricultural show in Camden, south of Sydney, with a representative from Guinness World Records present. After an exhibition of trick and fancy whip-cracking, the final act would be Gary's crack at the world record. Under the official rules, he would be allowed only one attempt.

The giant cowhide whip was laid out in a straight line on the ground, directly in front of a huge gathering of the show-going public. The arena announcers gave a full description of how 'the Australian Giant' was made, including its vital statistics: 42.27 metres long and weighing 22 kilos.

As the crowd held its collective breath, Gary gripped the 6-foot-long handle in both hands. Then he took off, running flat out toward the tip of the whip, dragging the bulk of it behind him. As he reached the halfway point, he suddenly reversed his run, causing the whip to form a huge loop in the air. At that point, the tip of the whip had risen well above the ground and was flying through the air at great speed. Pulling on the handle with all his might, Gary got the tip of the whip to 'snap'. He'd broken the sound barrier, at 343 metres per second, producing a crack that could be heard all over the showgrounds.

It is now recorded that Gary Brophy cracked the longest leather stockwhip in the world at the Camden Agricultural Show, New South Wales, Australia, on 3 March 1984.

From here on, the boys were on a roll, taking out record after record. Ashley's first was a world endurance record for tightwire walking, at the Adelaide Grand Prix in November 1985. For three and a half hours non-stop, he walked a tightwire (10 metres high), back and forth for 11.5 kilometres. This broke the previous world record held by Steven Wallenda, of the famous American family of wire walkers.

For New Year's Eve, 1985, Melbourne's Rialto Hotel booked Ashley to perform a Skywalk over their huge central courtyard, which resembled a piazza complete with outdoor settings. With hotel patrons packed into the courtyard below him, and fireworks all around, Ashley proceeded to walk 'the old year out and the new year in' along a 60-foot steel cable, five storeys above the crowd. He walked the wire without a net or any safety aids, to the thunderous applause of the revellers. Watching him walk that wire that night, I never felt nervous. I was, and still am, confident in his skills.

The following year, in Melbourne, Ashley claimed an unofficial world first on a tightwire erected on a moving vehicle. The wire was set up on a vehicle as part of the Moomba Parade. As the trailer was moving, often bouncing along the tram tracks, Ashley not only walked, he also skipped, danced and somersaulted his way along the wire with amazing dexterity, leaving onlookers awed for the entire three-kilometre parade.

In 1988, Ashley broke the existing record of fifty-eight skips on a tightwire using a skipping rope. He set a new world record, skipping 393 times non-stop, as recorded on the Channel Ten TV show *Just for the Record*.

To say Mick and I were proud of our boys and their achievements would be an understatement. With these world records under the boys' belts, we were ready for our second attempt at a full-scale circus.

In 1988, we moved all our vehicles to Sydney's Granville Showgrounds, an ideal area to make props and get the new circus ready to go on the road. Making the most of our old white tent until we could afford a bigger one, Mick – surprise, surprise – came up with a bright idea. Based on our fold-out caravan, he created a fold-out stage to go with our tent, with the whole lot built onto a five-tonne trailer.

At Granville, we met up with the Urban family, who were also camping at the showgrounds. The Urbans had come to Australia from Europe to work with Sole Bros Circus, as stunningly good trapeze artists. Gifted in all aspects of the circus arts, their biggest desire in life had been to own and run their own circus. For more than two years, in between performing in Sole's Circus, they had been stitching together hundreds of metres of canvas to form the roof of their full-scale circus tent. They battled hard, but despite all their expertise, they were feeling defeated and frustrated by a lack of funds. When we met them, they were at the end of their tether and wanting to return to Europe. After much discussion, we came to a fair deal and obtained their tent, which was perfect to fit on our now ready-to-travel stage trailer. (Little did I know that I would one day be using sections of this tent as the base on which to paint the showie history – let alone that my paintings would find their way into the National Library's Pandora Archive!)

Finally, we were ready to roll and moved onto our first site in Blacktown, Sydney. The Brophy Bros Variety Circus had arrived. And it really was a family affair once again. Joining us was Kym and her partner John, who came home to run the carnival out the front of our circus. Kym worked the canteen and John the games. Shayne, Wayne and our grandchildren had also arrived with their gaming stalls, but were mainly involved in performing in the show. It was wonderful to have all our lot together again, as this is what traditional circus is all about.

We now had a full crew to assist on the tent and a good team of performers, along with an advance agent who was already two weeks ahead of us doing the publicity and booking sites. Working places like Mount Druitt, Penrith and Glenmore Park gave us the time to iron out any kinks. The only problem was that Sydney had more than enough circuses working the suburbs, and they weren't too happy with new chums like us jumping into their territory. It was time to move out into the country.

With all our sons now licensed to drive heavy vehicles, a load was lifted from my shoulders. I could settle back and drive a station wagon instead of a heavy-duty truck! Up and over the Great Dividing Range we went, into Katoomba then on to Lithgow and Bathurst – normally very good circus towns. But it turned out that a rival circus, Harrison's, was only a few weeks ahead of us and had already worked these towns. Our advance man should have let us know. By the time we reached Moree, in northern New South Wales, Mick had found that Sole's Circus had left Sydney and were heading north through the New England area, while Lennon's Circus were heading up through Forbes and Dubbo, on their way to the Northern Territory. We were being surrounded! We were running out of areas to work, which meant we would soon be running out of money as well. With Queensland now out, our only option was to turn around and head south into Victoria, where we would probably freeze to death in the winter.

Before we left Moree, our advance man called it quits. Once again, Mick became the booking agent. Mick was now in his early sixties, with his health declining, but he was a stickler and never let on or complained.

Heading west to Collarenebri and down to Walgett, we eventually ended up in Deniliquin, near the border. Crossing into Victoria, we worked our way along the Murray River to Mildura, then doubled back through the centre of the state. Soon after we arrived in Bendigo, Mick became unwell. He started getting dizzy and confused, with blurry vision and massive headaches. When he started talking of a pounding in his chest and ears, it was off to hospital. There it was found his blood pressure had risen well beyond the limit. He was a candidate for heart failure or stroke. The specialist said Mick needed to stay put, at least until his health was brought under control. And even then, he would need ongoing care.

The boys and I had a sit-down conference. We needed a new plan, and quick. With Mick in hospital, we had no one to do the advance work, and to find someone qualified was almost impossible. We also needed more tent hands, as the boys were starting to feel the workload.

The long and short of it was that we had no choice but to shut down the full-scale circus temporarily. We would go back to working shopping centres. We were lucky at least that we were in the centre of Victoria, smack bang on all the major highways. So, we could easily head off in any direction to work, with Bendigo as our base.

That was that. Our next step was to find permanent quarters to live in and store our surplus equipment. We couldn't pay out dead money in rent each month; we would be better off buying a property.

With all our staff and performers settled into work with other circuses, Shayne and Wayne settled on a place in Neilborough, a mining and farming area 25 kilometres west of Bendigo. (A few years later they built a beautiful brick home and set up a canteen at the Bendigo markets, selling hamburgers, chips and hot jam donuts every Sunday, which they operate to this day.)

When Mick eventually got out of hospital, it was a constant battle to stop him from doing any heavy work. I gave him the job of finding a property for the two of us, while I spent most of my time contacting various organisations to obtain future bookings of the Brophy Bros Circus Attractions.

When Mick found a property near Shayne and Wayne's, we jumped at it, especially as it had a huge hay shed that was ideal for storage. Mick loved his new home. It was his decision as to what would be built and where. I do believe it was instrumental in getting him back on his feet as he carefully arranged to have the huge hay shed fully walled in and divided into parking compartments for the vehicles and our caravans.

Over the next couple of years, we made many changes to our lives, while our three sons ran the circus attractions at various venues. Eventually we built a three-bedroom house up the front of the property, complete with a huge lounge room and log fireplace. Outside was a fire pit built into a seating area, in the centre of our tropical garden, where we entertained the many show people who came to visit.

It took some time, but the garden became a showpiece, featuring palm trees brought down from the north of Queensland and a huge goldfish pond complete with a waterfall and bridge to stroll over. Mick was so proud of the place.

At a glance, it looked like we were becoming locals. But once a showie always a showie, and that applied to our kids too.

Chapter 28

Next Generation

Late 1980s to present

As Mick and I settled into our new home and life, we discovered it was Kym's turn to come up with a bright idea for the family business. She wanted to know what we intended to do with our big van, which was now in storage. Could she have it to turn into a food van, to work on the agricultural show circuit? Kym was always a great cook, so we knew this would work great.

In no time, we had a canteen ready to go, named Fu-Man-Choo Take-Away. Below the serving counter, I painted a fire-breathing dragon along the full length of the van. The boys did a great job of stripping the inside and rebuilding the kitchen.

As a new mum (baby Elliot was born in September 1988) and a canteen chef, Kym was in her element. Not only did she now have the son she had always dreamed of, she was also earning a living doing what she did best: cooking good food for the hungry hordes on show days. But as popular as the Chinese food was, Kym felt she could do better if she concentrated more on the show staff. In 1989, after building in extra refrigeration, grill plates and ovens, Kym opened her first full-scale café diner to feed showies seven days a week. The Showman's Guild allocated her a position in each showground's camping area, which would also be accessible for the staff on show days.

With the old showie Teddy Trevor operating his long-running breakfast café for showies, Kym could work the afternoons and nights. There was even a campfire for staff to gather around into the late evening. Like Mick and I with our fire pit, Kim was recreating the old scenarios of the showies meeting around the campfire, just like in my dad's day and my youth. Such moments were precious – a time for showies to share a yarn and brainstorm new ideas in an industry that was, and is, always facing challenges.

(In later years, thanks to a cookhouse caravan that Gary found, Kym could have as many as sixty diners eating at the same time. This van had been built by long-time circus man Bert Weber to use as a back-of-house eatery for the staff of *Cats*, when the musical toured Australia in the 1990s. For over thirty years, Kym was to cook for not only the staff but also for many of the showfolk and their children. All the kids knew her as Aunty Kym, with the majority forgetting to pay for their soft drinks. Kym was always a soft touch.)

During these years, Gary did some TV bookings through the Victorian agency of Malcolm Haslett, who found that there was a spot for a high-wire walker in a TV advertisement for MLC

Insurance. The client didn't want Ashley, as they felt he looked too young for the part. So Gary, who had never walked wire in his life, paid Ashley to teach him. This TV commercial went over so well that it was extended for a further year.

Gary, aged twenty-four, followed this up by creating and performing his own half-hour exhibitions known as 'Gary Brophy's Wild West Show'. Ready to go it alone, he loaded up a truck and caravan with a newly built and sign-written set-up for his show, created by me, of course. He also had his giant whip on display, along with all the paraphernalia to complete his one-man show. With a run of shopping centres to work, he was now his own man, starting his first run on the coast north of Sydney and including some agricultural shows and festivals.

In this way, Gary could be near his fiancée, Caroline Belli, of the world-renowned Belli circus family. The Bellis can authenticate their heritage back fourteen generations. Having performed before many of Europe's royal families, and throughout two world wars, they are believed to represent the longest continuous family line of circus artists in the world.

While Gary was away, the younger Brophy men were flat out themselves, working in shopping centres and show arenas. Ashley and Warren put together a 20-minute high-wire and high-jinx stunt show incorporating their old 'Clowning Around' act, with Warren performing as the bumbling, stumbling clown Wazza on both the tiny and the giant unicycles. They mostly worked their show within driving distance of home with us, while I managed their bookings for them.

It was around this time that Warren and Ashley heard of an act for sale. The high-wire motorbike stunt rider Robert Bugler was heading back to Europe, and the cost of transporting all of his equipment was too much. He asked Warren and Ashley if they might be interested. The boys immediately took up the offer.

With Gary offering to come home to give his brothers a hand, and Shayne keen to organise a trapeze act, it was all systems go for the new show. Mick and I couldn't just sit back and watch. We were going to be needed on the road as well. So much for settling down! The Brophys were back together. And we might as well go out with a big bang. It was time for The Flying Angels High-Wire Motorbike Stunt Show!

The boys spent months working on their stunts. In the back paddock at our place, they set up a cable between two giant gum trees. They then attached the special motorbike and slowly got the hang of how to perform this dangerous high-wire act. Motorists passing by our property were amazed at the spectacle of a motorbike, 50 feet in the air, whizzing past them. Our property soon became the number one tourist attraction in the area.

Meantime, Shayne worked flat out training two truly wonderful sisters, Annette and Shari Burch, to perform as trapeze artists for the finale to the act. The girls lived in the area with their farming parents. They had never performed trapeze but were willing to learn. They practised day after day, with Shayne pushing them to the limit on twin trapeze bars hanging from the centre struts in our big shed. It was essential that the girls co-ordinated their timing with each other as they would both be performing at the same time, up to 30 metres off the ground.

A friend of the boys, Jason Nocen, joined in on the act as a clown. Every act needs a clown, particularly to distract the audience while the act is being set up. And Jason was a bit of a clown in real life. A showman's son, he adored the Brophy brothers from the first time he spied them riding on their minibikes as a youngster. Jason was forever ringside. For years, he was pretty much another son to me. It was only right that he was part of this all-family act.

When Gary returned home to help out, he dug out a pair of fibreglass carousel horses, which we had stored some years before. They would form part of the finale known as 'The Flying Angels on the Carousel in the Sky'.

As our Flying Angels would be the only motorbike act to ever have four people risking their lives on a single motorbike, Mick had his work cut out as safety officer. He'd done this for all our acts over the years. Even though he wasn't mechanically minded, when it came to his kids, he was very aware of what could go wrong, and how to prevent it. But this time around, there would be no room for error whatsoever. Carrying almost half a tonne of equipment, with performers up to 33 metres in the air on a slender steel cable attached to a giant crane, this act was a truly terrifying world-first. Be it a success or disaster, we knew it was going to make one hell of an impact.

Our highly publicised act was to premiere at Melbourne's 1987 Moomba Festival. The high-wire spanned the Yarra River, with a

75-tonne crane to hold the cable taut. Crowds thronged on both sides of the river in anticipation.

After Mick had checked over the boys' set-up, he sat down with me to enjoy the act. We weren't concerned for the safety of our 'kids'. You had to clear your mind of any thoughts of 'could be's' and 'maybes'. In this business you were aware that plenty could go wrong. The trick was to do all you could to ensure it didn't, and then just forget about it. Your mind must be clear.

Warren checked his bike at the start of the cable just above the ground, ready for his first run up the cable. Meanwhile, Jason the crazy clown clowned around under the motorbike, keeping the children in the audience entertained. He was wearing an enormously colourful clown shirt, giving the appearance of being a very fat clown. When Warren caught sight of Jason trying to grab the undercarriage of the bike, he shook a fist at him. Laughs all round, but then the bike suddenly took off, with Jason hanging on for dear life. Jason's 10-metre-long shirt was 'accidentally' dragged from him and, like a colourful streamer, was now floating high in the sky, with skinny little Jason dangling beneath the bike, wearing only his tiny undies. All this created lots of laughter before the events that were about to unfold.

It was now Ashley's turn. He mounted an Australian flag on the rear of the bike, then performed a series of incredibly dangerous handstands as Warren once again drove up the cable. Fireworks exploded all around the two daredevils, to the wild applause of the huge audience.

Perched on the cable over the Yarra, Warren now locked his bike in place. He dismounted, climbing down to join Ashley on the huge revolving ladder underneath. They performed a breathtaking stunt as the ladder revolved, turning over and over at great speed, with Warren on one end and Ashley on the other, neither wearing any safety devices.

For the final stunt, the revolving ladder was transformed into a hair-raising merry-go-round. With our two carousel horses clamped to each end of the ladder, swaying backwards and forwards, our beautiful young trapeze artists Annette and Sharron climbed aboard a horse each for a stunning display of high-wire balancing and twirling.

The Moomba Festival had never seen anything like it.

From that day on, the Flying Angels performed in most large towns and major cities on the mainland and Tasmania. Warren and Ashley took it all in their stride, but they had achieved the almost impossible and were stars in their own right.

Our pride in the whole family was immense but, as parents, we knew we had to let go of the apron strings. We had to allow the next generation to run their own lives. Having achieved a dream together, it was time for Mick and I to bow out. So, following the Albury show in March 1989, we closed the Brophy Bros Circus Attractions, and the highly dangerous Flying Angels Highwire Motorbike Act, for good.

Ashley went on to compete in the Circus World Championships in Paris, at the Festival Mondial du Cirque de Domain. This annual competition is an invitation-only event for elite circus artists worldwide. In 1991, Ashley's solo performance of tightwire walking was awarded fourth place. First place went to a troupe of ten tumblers from China. Ashley was the only solo performer in the competition. This has led Ashley to become a sought-after performer, working for renowned circuses all over the world.

Warren went on to join Perry Bros Circus, and marry Yasmin Maynard, the great-great-granddaughter of the original Perry. Thirty years later, he and Yasmin's eldest son, 'Wokka', is following the family tradition. He now runs his own stunt shows as Brophy Entertainment, travelling throughout the world. In 2018, he performed in Kazakhstan on the Wheel of Death.

When Gary and Caroline got married, they left Australia for Switzerland. There they joined Circus Royale, managed by Danny Gasser, husband to Rose Belli. After their return from an extensive tour of Europe, Gary and Caroline eventually opened their own circus, 'Circus Sunrise', with other members of Caroline's family. Many years later, their gun-twirling, whip-cracking daughter Jessinta holds a number of records for rope spinning.

Chapter 29

Sadness and Surprises

2005 to present

Sadly, the great Mick Brophy passed away in 2005, on the morning of Melbourne Cup Day.

My incredible husband and I were fortunate to have had fifty wonderful years together. He was my backbone and my strength. The most loving partner in the world, he showed me nothing but care and devotion in so many ways throughout all of those exciting and challenging times.

Between us, we became proud grandparents of thirteen grandchildren through our biological children. Shayne is the mother of two boys and one girl. Kym has one son. Gary has two daughters and Warren has three sons. Ashley, our youngest, married a trapeze artist and show dancer named Rochelle and they have one girl. Their marriage wasn't to last, and some years later Ashley met Michelle Scott (Mina). They now have two boys and one girl.

And then we have Mick's two sons, Michael and Fred, from his first marriage, each having had eight children. Our family tree stretches further still, and we love each and every one on it. Counting the whole 'clan' to date, we have sixty-eight grandchildren and great-grandchildren.

But there was one branch that certainly came as a surprise. Do you remember that secret Florence kept to herself when she left Tasmania all those years ago, after the death of her third child? Well, that secret came to be revealed to us back in the late 1980s.

One day, I received a phone call from a lady named Geraldine Perkins. She had been given my number after a chance meeting with a circus man, John McDonald.

Geraldine, with two of her siblings, arrived at my home well-armed with photos and documents. Over the next few hours, it came out that her biological parents had been circus people. Her adoptive parents, Fam and Mary Chenall, had never kept it a secret as to why she was given away.

Her biological mother, Philda, was the baby of Bert and Florence. Philda was the baby who had supposedly died at birth in 1914, while my father Bert was working on the mainland and Florence, at only nineteen, was living in Launceston with their two tiny children. The story goes that with the birth imminent, Florence was panic stricken. How was she going to cope with three babies and a husband who was away most of the time? The midwife made a suggestion. She knew of a lady who only hours earlier had given birth to a stillborn baby girl and was heartbroken. The grief-stricken woman would gladly take Florence's baby. And that's what she did.

On Bert's arrival home, Florence didn't dare tell him that she had given the baby away. My father went to his grave never knowing his daughter, Philda Gertrude Chenall, was still alive – let alone that she had grown to be a happily married woman with seven children.

Philda had never stopped searching for her birth parents, approaching every circus and showman that came to Tasmania. But she was only ever met with a wall of silence.

In 1989, just three months before her demise at age seventy-six, Philda was fortunate enough to take a trip to New Zealand, where she met her full-blood sister Edna, the last of her birth family that Philda had spent over fifty years searching for.

I am forever grateful for Geraldine's chance meeting with John McDonald, as I now have another side to my family that has become particularly special to me.

Epilogue – For the Show People

When I look back over my life, I see a woman who has done it all with the help of my stubbornness and hard-headedness. I never expected anything to be handed to me on a silver platter. I worked. I busted a gut and put in the hours, leaving nothing to chance. I taught myself to tackle the near impossible. In doing so, I knew that I could pass on to my family the knowledge that everything they do in life could be handled, even if it seems to have no reward at the time.

Showies aren't known for their sentimentality. We often stuff our feelings down to get the job done. But here I will say that my heart swells with pride at the sheer guts and achievements of my forefathers, my family and my peers in the industry.

While my memoir is a family history, it is also my way of capturing this important part of Australian history: the life of the outdoor entertainment industry and its people. The clowns. The trapeze artists. The stunt riders. The singers. The dancers. The tightwire walkers. The sideshow alley operators. The actors.

The tease girls. The sharpshooters. The caterers. The fairy floss men and women. And so many more. May they live forevermore, to entertain, shock, tickle your fancy, and give you a chance to pause and dream.

At the time of writing, the world is recovering from the COVID-19 pandemic and its fallout, which hit the outdoor entertainment industry hard, like so many others. All the shows and circuses were cancelled. Hundreds of self-employed families were out of work. I know that, like the generations of show people before them, my people will recover. They are resilient. They are creative. They will think of new ways of re-inventing themselves. And I know, without a shadow of a doubt, they will rise to enthral and amaze the 'townies' once again.

To my people, the show people, I am proud of you. I am proud of us.

Acknowledgements

To Karen Tyrrell, Brisbane writer and speaker, who I met at Logan Artists Association. Thank you for encouraging me to write my story and for suggesting I contact Wendy Stuart for editorial support.

To Wendy Stuart. You became not only my co-writer and editor, but more importantly, a good friend. Thanks for your patience and hard work, and for your naughty humour at times. I think we did a great job together. A special thanks to Wendy's husband, Peter Stuart, for his chauffeuring and giving his two bob's worth while enjoying my massage chair and the company of my dog, Mr Fu.

To Martin Hughes, Publishing Director of Affirm Press, thank you for believing in my story and recognising the value of the lives of the outdoor entertainment people. Thanks for being a fellow dreamer. A nod also to Affirm's Managing Editor Kevin O'Brien for overseeing final editing and to Mic Looby, Contracting Editor, for taking our manuscript to the next level. Overall a great team to journey with.

To the Pandora Archive of the National Library of Australia, thank you for regarding my paintings of show history as national treasures and archiving my website forever to be enjoyed by future generations. Your recognition gave me great encouragement to write and publish this book.

To my children, Shayne, Kym, Gary, Warren and Ashley, thanks for finally reading my book and for your input. Thanks for supporting me in my twilight years and giving me the time I needed to write this story. Without you, there wouldn't be a story.